Elvis

Elvis Presley was rock's first superstar.
He was rock's first sex symbol.
Rock's first rebel.
Rock's first great innovator.
He was rock's first stylist.

Everything, everyone that followed owed a debt to him. Without Elvis rock & roll would have been a passing, short-lived fad. Without him there would never have been teenagers, greased-back hair, drape clothes, sneering lips, wiggling hips. Presley was the first and one of the very few rock figures that has ever equalled in fame and popularity the magic of Hollywood superstars in the golden age. He was to the '50s what Clark Gable had been to the '30s and Bogart to the '40s. He outsold, out-filmed, out-rocked, outraged more people than any rock star ever. This is the story of one of the most famous men of our century, and one of the least known. The story of a career that heralded the rock & roll era and took Elvis Presley from humble beginnings in America's poor South to the peaks of international stardom. The story of his hits, his films, his triumphs, his wealth and his tragic death. It is the story of an enigmatic figure who survived in the most ephemeral and fickle of worlds. It is the story of the King and his court.

**Written by
Dick Tatham**

**Edited and film material
written by Jeremy Pascall
Designed by Rob Burt**

We are indebted to the Official Elvis Presley Fan Club of Great Britain, PO Box 4, Leicester, for their help in the compilation of this publication and for many of the photographs.

© 1977 Phoebus Publishing Company/
BPC Publishing Limited
169 Wardour Street, London W1A 2JX

Part published in *Elvis* © 1976/1977
Phoebus Publishing Company/BPC Publishing
Limited

Filmsetting and reproduction by
Petty & Sons Ltd, Leeds.
Made and printed in Great Britain by
Waterlow (Dunstable) Limited

ISBN 0 7026 0014 8

CONTENTS

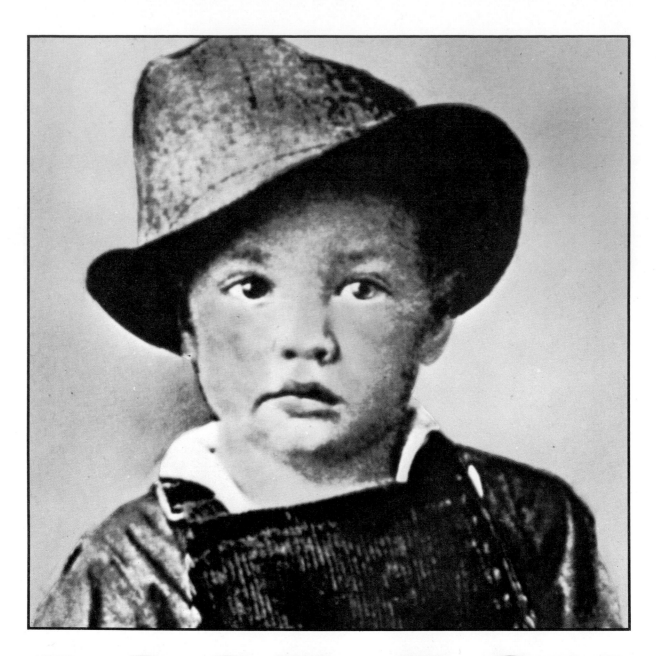

POOR BOY

For Vernon and Gladys Presley, this day was to be different. Even before he could walk, they had started taking Elvis to the First Assembly of God church. It was a small, simple, wooden structure on Adams Street, Tupelo, Mississippi, that rang with the fervent worship of its Holy Roller congregations. They had noticed before that Elvis had taken to clapping his hands in time to the singing. But on this day in 1938, when he was three, he did more. He slid from his mother's knee, toddled down the aisle and scrambled onto the choir platform.

"I let him stay on the platform," his mother recalled years later. "He was coming to no harm and wasn't bothering anyone. He got into the habit of doing this.

He would look up to the choir and try to sing with them. He was too young to know the words but he could keep to the tune."

It was a humble enough setting for the first musical achievement of Elvis Presley — and, indeed, the whole background of the phenomenon that was Elvis was as humble as a potato patch.

His parents came from modest stock. Vernon Presley had grown up on a farm in Tupelo — the tradition-conscious cotton town where Presleys had lived for over a century. Gladys was one of eight children. Their father had died when she was 12 and since then she had worked on the land with the others, chopping corn and picking cotton. The couple were married in 1933, at which time Vernon was working on a

farm with his father and Gladys had recently become a garment factory machinist.

They lived at first with her parents — the Smiths. Then they moved in with Vernon's parents. That summer, finding she was pregnant, Gladys quit her job. Vernon had by then switched to delivering milk and groceries door-to-door and because he was now going to need a home of his own, his boss rented him a shack he owned, a simple structure with only two rooms and an outside toilet. It was on piles of brick and concrete to guard against floods and the mud which often sludged down from the hillside nearby.

The doctors had told Gladys she would have twins. She and Vernon decided in advance on their names: Elvis Aaron and Jesse Garon. Gladys Presley gave birth in the early afternoon of January 8, 1935. Jesse was born dead. By evening, he was laid in a coffin in the front room and the next day he was buried in an unmarked grave in the local cemetery. The Presleys had no more children.

Mississippi is liable to extremes of climate — summer droughts contrasting with wet winters beset by hurricanes blowing up from the Gulf of Mexico. At the time Elvis was born, it was also an area badly hit by America's economic Depression. "I could say we lived on the wrong side of the tracks," said Elvis when everyone had become eager to know all about him. "But in those days in Tupelo, there wasn't really a right side of the tracks. No one was eating too good. We never starved but we were close to it at times. There were plenty of times I thought, 'Please, God, don't let us stay in these conditions forever.' But when I was in the old church, singing with my mother and father — that was when I forgot about the problems."

Keen to spur their small son's clear zeal for singing, his parents formed a trio with him with Vernon and Elvis singing and Gladys playing mouth organ. They performed hymns and other religious songs at church conventions, revivalist meetings and religious camps.

Moral Fiber

Neither Vernon nor Gladys had been able to complete their formal education and they admitted their reading and writing was slow, but whatever they lacked academically, they atoned for in moral fiber. They wanted to bring up Elvis well. As Mrs. Presley once recalled: "We didn't go to school much because we had to work. Vernon quit in the fifth grade to help in the cotton fields. That was why we wanted, above all, for our son to get an education and learn a good trade." Partly because of this — and also, no doubt, because of a natural urge to protect their only surviving child — they cloistered him somewhat in his early boyhood.

"In Tupelo," he once said, "I was never allowed out of the yard. All the kids would go swimming in the creek. But Mama wouldn't let me join them. That's why I never learned to swim as a kid and I'm not much good now. Nor would Mama let me go roughing around with the local gangs of kids. She was awful scared I might get hurt. Being her only child, I didn't argue. My folks were strict and I guess I champed the bit at times but I don't regret having missed all the tearing around with other kids. My folks' strictness in bringing me up was the best thing that ever happened to me, though I didn't realize it then."

From a very early age, Elvis was receptive to music. Church music came first and his favorite hymn for years was 'I Won't Have To Cross Jordan Alone'. But then came the music of local folk. In their stale, lustreless lot of the Depression days, they would seek solace in singing hillbilly favorites and railroad blues while picking at beat-up guitars. Elvis would absorb the raw feel and compulsive rhythms of these songs.

One of the first clear signs of the young Presley's performing potential came when he was nine years old and in the fifth grade of his Tupelo school. His teacher, Mrs. JC Grimes reported to Gladys. "Two mornings we asked for a child to come up in front of assembly and say a prayer. No one did. But on the third day, Elvis came up," she said. "He said a prayer *and* sang several songs. One was 'Old Shep'. Maybe it's not exactly the song for assembly service, but it made me cry."

'Old Shep'

Gladys Presley excitedly gave the news to her husband while Mrs. Grimes passed the word to school principal JD Cole. Not long after, he sent Mrs. Presley a note saying that the Alabama-Mississippi fair was due and there would be the usual amateur singing contest. If it was all right with her, they would like to enter Elvis. It was, of course, all right with her.

"I'll never forget that day," she was to recall years later. "When I took Elvis up on the platform, we had a problem about accompaniment. Elvis had no guitar and the kids who did, wouldn't play for him. They didn't want to help a rival. Also, Elvis wasn't tall enough to reach the microphone, so we got a chair for him to stand on and he sang 'Old Shep' unaccompanied. We were thrilled that Elvis was able to sing like that in front of thousands of people." That day, the voice which was to make millions had its first reward: second prize of $5 plus free admission to the sideshows.

Some time later, in early January, 1945, Elvis and his mother stood looking in the window of the Tupelo store. "Elvis . . . You *sure* it's a bicycle you want? That looks a mighty fine guitar just there. You wouldn't sooner have that?" The boy's eyes lit up. "That's a great idea. . . . I need a guitar if I'm gonna be a singer." Elvis's tenth birthday was near and his folks knew he wanted a bicycle, but they also knew that they couldn't afford the $55 it would cost. The guitar was $12.95 and it was soon clear that Mrs. Presley's bright idea was to have a result much more important than saving money. Learning to play the guitar became *the* thing in Elvis's life.

He couldn't read music — nor did he ever get around to it — but he eagerly learned chords from his uncles Vester Presley and Johnny Smith, and he would sit endlessly by the radio — singing and playing along with the country performers. Meantime, through church visits twice a week, he was developing a deep feel for spirituals, and by singing and playing at church and lay events in the Tupelo area, he began to fashion his own performing style.

A New Life

But the Presley family remained bogged in poverty and there didn't seem any prospect of things getting better where they were. Elvis always remembered the night when his father said: "I don't want to leave Tupelo. I've lived here man and boy and this is where my roots are, but I've decided it's time to start a new life."

"For a long time we had dreamed of making a move," he recalled years later.

Left: Elvis Aaron at about two years old. Below: ties with his parents were close.

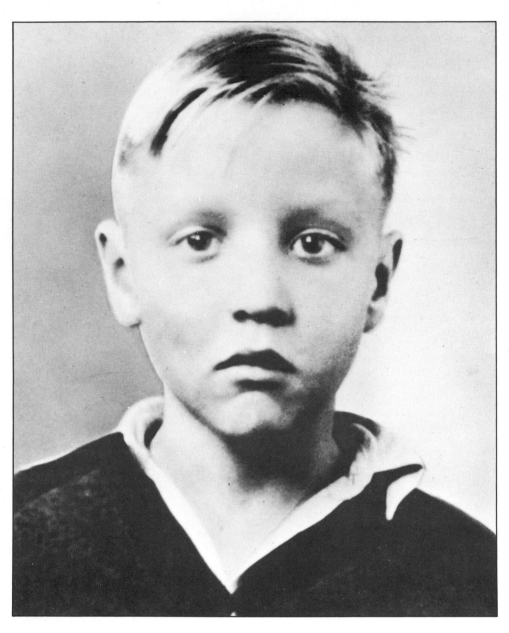

Elvis, aged six. He dyed his natural reddish-brown hair to black early in his career.

Late the next year, Elvis became a cinema usher at Loew's State Theater. He worked nightly from five till ten for $14 a week but his mother made him quit after a few weeks because his studies were suffering. He returned, however, when his 1951 summer holidays started. But shortly after, he was fired because another usher had gone to the management with a story that the girl selling sweets and popcorn had been giving some to Elvis — and Elvis had hit him.

Elvis was still intent on helping his parents — especially since his mother's ill health had forced her to leave the cafeteria — and he signed on with the local Marl Metal Products Company for a spare time shift. Predictably, he began dozing off at school and again his mother made him quit. Despite her poor health, she went back to work at a local hospital.

Internal Strife

In these years of his mid-teens, Elvis's character was being shaped. Within him, opposing influences clashed. There was the strict, principled, courteous outlook taught by his parents. And there was the age-old rebellion of youth — eager for expression at a time when the first ripples of teenage revolt were spreading across the States, inspired in no small way by movie actor James Dean. Talking about his teenage outlooks, Elvis once revealed: "I began looking for excitement. You soon get bored with it. You start looking for something else. That's when you've got to be careful. You get so bored you feel you have to do something and without really trying to, you can get into all sorts of trouble.

"I admit I occasionally thought of being evil and getting into trouble just for kicks, but I managed to keep myself in check. I once even wanted to run away from home — I guess all kids do — but I stopped myself in time. It took me a long while to start listening to people who knew more than I did and to accept their advice. Till then, I always thought I knew what was best for me but I had a heck of a lot to learn, as I realized later."

Above all, Elvis obeyed his mother. He gave up football at Humes High because she was scared he would get hurt. He shunned smoking and drinking because she said they would be bad for him. "I was brought up real right," he once recalled. "I was taught that if you are bad, you certainly go to hell and if you're good, you stand some kinda chance of going to heaven. It's a simple philosophy but a mighty fine one. My Mom made sure I was always polite, she didn't like my arguing. Said there was never any need for it and if you can't speak good about someone, say nothing. Mom was a good woman. Best there's ever been."

Inevitably, once Elvis was famous, writers asked his former teachers about him. As Mrs. Eleanor Richmond said: "He was a gracious, quiet boy and we were all aware of his deep religious convictions." And this was supported by

"We figured if we went to Memphis there would be more money and it would be more fun for Elvis, but in the early days we were bitterly disappointed. His mother and I walked the streets looking for work. We did this even in heavy rain or snow but for quite a time, there was no work to be found. My wife and I tried to keep our troubles from Elvis, but he was sensitive and I'm sure he knew what was happening, even if we didn't talk about our problems out loud."

The family's move from Tupelo to Memphis took place on September 16, 1948. They had sold their few bits of furniture and with their modest belongings stacked inside and on top of their beat-up 1939 Plymouth, they drove 100 miles north to Memphis.

For Elvis, it was a stark change of setting. The sleepy, homely atmosphere of Tupelo was replaced by the gaudy, bustling life of the big city. At the LC Humes High School where Elvis was enrolled, there were over 1600 students — more than the whole population of East Tupelo! Vernon Presley at last found a

job — poorly paid — with a tool making firm but expenses, luckily, were low. The Presleys' first Memphis home was at 572 Poplar Avenue, a large house which had been converted into 16 one-room dwellings. In their single room, the Presleys lived, slept and ate while their water came from the communal bathroom. They cooked on a hot plate. However, they made the best of their lot despite the skimped heating and the room's drab decor.

Doggedly the family struggled for something better. Vernon bettered his wages by changing jobs — becoming a truck driver for a grocery firm and later a packer with a paint company. Gladys dispensed coffee at a downtown cafeteria, and worked in a curtain factory. Elvis began mowing lawns, cleaning cars and doing other sparetime chores. Things improved slowly though and after nearly a year in Memphis, the family found a better home — in Lauderdale Court on Winchester Street — which was owned by the Memphis authorities, who rented the apartments only to low-income families.

the memory of Miss Susie Johnson, who said: "Elvis was gentle, obedient and religious with a warm, likable disposition." It seems that they were voicing the general view.

As if to compensate for the way he conformed in behavior, Elvis went into revolt with his appearance. The Memphis youths of the day sported conventional clothes and GI crewcuts. Elvis decided this wasn't him. Being shy and mistrustful of the big city, he had drawn into himself and been wary of his fellow students, but when he was 16 he felt it was time he stood out and much against his parents' wishes, he grew his hair long — heaping grease on it and combing it into a dangling curve at the front and a duck's ass at the back. He added huge sideburns and he began dressing in black. He explained years later: "I wanted to be different — to look older and be noticed. The only way I could do it was with long hair, sideburns and black clothes. I took a lot of kidding from my friends, but I stuck to it."

His fascination for stand-out clothes was something he could satisfy only in a small way while doing part-time jobs — but once he had left school and was working full time, he stepped things up. One place he would go was Lansky's Clothing Emporium on Beale Street. Bernard Lansky once added his memories to those of other locals: "We'd always have a good display of clothes in the window and time after time I'd see this tall, lanky boy hanging around and pressing his nose to the glass, like a kid at a candy store. Lots of times I'd say, 'Elvis — come on in and let me fit you out with something real snazzy.' He would show me his empty pockets and reply, 'No, sir. I ain't got nothing. But one day, I'm gonna buy you out.' When he got a job after school, he began to buy here. Always for cash. I never saw anyone so crazy over clothes. When he began to click as a singer, he really did buy us out. Our whole stock went on him, his relatives and friends."

Heartbreak

During his last year at Humes High, Elvis dated a senior student named Billie, who was a part-time waitress. He later remembered her as "two years older, taller and heavier than me. But I believed she was the most beautiful creature on God's earth. She would listen to me sing and play guitar and say I was real good, but she found somebody else and it broke my heart."

Elvis had few dates as a student — mainly because he had little money. He recalls sitting on the front steps at Lauderdale Court — watching the passing cars and dreaming of the day when he would buy a Cadillac for his parents and another for himself. And, increasingly, it was becoming clear to him that the one way he *might* make a fortune fast was through his singing. He would perform

The future star aged eight with his parents at Tupelo, their first home.

Aged 13 posing in an elaborate cowboy outfit.

Elvis the adolescent with his cousin, Gene Smith.

A foretaste of *GI Blues,* Elvis in the cadet force.

An archetypal teenager, complete with acne.

at school in variety shows, at assembly and during lunch breaks, and it was at school, in his last year, that a proud moment came when, because there were so many performers for the big annual show, the teacher in charge said there would be only one encore — by the singer who gained most applause. That singer was Elvis — with his rendering of the country favorite 'Cold Cold Icy Fingers'.

Early in 1953 Elvis graduated, without honors, from Humes High. After a brief spell in a tool factory, he applied for a job with the Crown Electric Company, which did electrical contract work for firms, schools, shops, houses and so on. It employed 45 electricians and two truck drivers who ran the electrical gear to where it was needed. One of the driving jobs had fallen vacant and Elvis was given it at $35 a week. Also, it was arranged that he would study at evening school with a view to becoming an electrician.

Vocal Gift

As he drove the Crown Electric truck through Memphis his eye was caught by the Memphis Recording Service which announced that people could have weddings or other personal events recorded as souvenirs. Also, aspiring singers could make private discs. This alerted Elvis's interest and he decided to spend a few dollars to make a recording for his mother's coming birthday.

This was to initiate a momentous series of events because the Memphis Recording Service was a subsidiary of The Sun Record Company.

Sun had been launched in 1950 by Sam Phillips and his brother Judd who at first had concentrated mainly on recording black blues and R&B singers and leasing or selling the tapes to bigger disc firms for release. But at the start of 1953 they began releasing some of the material on their own Sun label.

One day in June, the same year, Judd Phillips happened to notice a tall, rangy kid carrying a guitar standing hesitantly by the entrance when he came out for a late morning coffee. When he came back 30 minutes later, the kid was still there — leaning against a lamp post. "He was a shaggy-looking country boy with dark hair and long sideburns," Phillips later remembered. "He seemed so agitated, I went up and asked if I could help." Judd suggested that Elvis go up and see Marion Keisker.

Marion was impressed. The kid was only halfway through his first song but already she sensed he had something. She was a woman in her thirties who had done radio work since she was a child and her judgement was based on professional experience. At that time — the mid-summer of 1953 — she was office manager at Sun Records.

The boy had come up to the first-floor studio around 12.30 clutching his guitar and he was clearly as taut as its strings. "I thought," she was to recall a few years later, "that he was a drifter looking for a handout. He wore dirty khaki clothes, his hair was long and his face was dirty." Hesitantly he had stated his business: "I'd like to make a private record. I've been hanging around outside the best part of an hour. Sorta scared. A gentleman just told me not to be scared but to come on up. Name of Judd Phillips. Said he was one of the bosses here." In exchange for $4 Marion Keisker helped him cut a disc of 'My Happiness' and 'That's When Your Heartaches Begin'.

She decided to make a tape of Elvis midway through 'My Happiness' because she thought Sam Phillips ought to hear the singer when he got back from lunch. But as it happened, Phillips came back while Elvis was still there. He listened to the tape and told Elvis he had promise. He wrote down his name and work number and with this encouragement and vague hopes for the future Elvis paid for the session and went off with his disc. Years later he was to say of it: "I was terrible. I had wanted to hear how I sounded because I'd been listening to discs a long time and whenever I'd heard a good singer I'd say, 'I hate him!' After making that first record, I went on doing that."

Whatever ambition the young Presley may have had to be a professional musician was undoubtedly spurred by necessity. One night in 1953 his father came home from work evidently wracked with pain as the result of a back complaint. Elvis and his mother rushed with Vernon to the hospital, where the doctor's verdict was that he had a slipped disc which would confine him to the hospital for a couple of weeks. But even when he was allowed home, Vernon wasn't fit for work and mostly he was forced to remain in bed. After several weeks of this, Elvis came home one evening to find his father sitting on the bed with his head in his hands.

A Father's Tears

"Till that night, I hadn't realized our position was getting serious," Elvis recalled a few years later. "I asked Dad what the trouble was and he told me, 'It's time you knew the truth. My back is worse than I thought. I'll probably be off work for long periods. We'll have a job making ends meet.' Then he gave a series of short, quick sobs. I'd never known my father to cry. I didn't know a grown man could cry."

During this period Elvis was also concerned about his mother's health. In her case, there was no critical moment of illness, but clearly she was frail from years of dogged work and frequent deprivation. His parents' condition spurred him to help in whatever way he could and there is little doubt that in the early months of 1954 he must have seen with growing clarity the road he had to take. If he could somehow hit it big as a singer, he could both fulfil his ambition to get somewhere and to be somebody and, at the same time, lift his parents from their sombre, stinted way of life.

In April, 1954, he returned to the Sun studios and this time he recorded 'Casual Love' and 'I'll Never Stand In Your Way'. Again Marion Keisker was impressed. Again Sam told Elvis he had promise and that he might be in touch. Again nothing concrete was decided.

A few weeks later, however, Sam had a problem. He was always getting demonstration discs and he received one of a song he liked called 'Without You'. He wanted to release it and he started phoning around to find out who the singer was. When he had no luck, he told Marion Keisker: "This is a great song and if I don't locate the singer soon, I'll get someone else to do it." Marion suggested that they get Elvis.

Phillips phoned Elvis at Crown Electric and the singer ran eagerly to Sun. Sam set aside three hours of studio time but Elvis's efforts to put down a saleable recording of the song were clearly a flop. Nothing daunted, Phillips decided it was worth persevering with Elvis and he called in two experienced country musicians to work with him: guitarist Scotty Moore and bassman Bill Black. Throughout that June, night after night, the three worked on country songs — making demos for Sam to consider.

Black & White

Progress wasn't easy and as Black was later to recall of his teaming with Elvis: "I don't think either of us was much impressed by the other at the start but all we had was one another. Then we found our sense of rhythm matched. Rhythm was what Elvis went by. When he had the right rhythm, we knew we were close to what was wanted."

At the time, the Phillips brothers were aware of the growing interest of American youth in black music. They were sure there were big commercial possibilities for white singers with a black sound. They realized if they could get the right sound from Elvis, then this plus his youth plus his smouldering good looks could prove a powerful mix.

This idea prompted what was to be a vital development which Elvis once enthusiastically described in an interview: "Sam phoned one day and asked, 'You

want to make some blues?' He knew I'd always been a sucker for that kind of jive. He mentioned Arthur "Big Boy" Crudup and maybe other names. I don't remember. I was so excited I hung up and ran the 15 blocks to Sam's office. I was with him before he'd gotten off the line! We talked about the Crudup records I knew like 'Cool Disposition', 'Rock Me Mamma', 'Hey Mama', 'Everything's All Right' and one of my top favorites, 'That's All Right (Mama)'. Sam said we should try recording some of them and I was real excited."

But if Sam's aim for a sound was deliberate the exact moment of its fashioning came by accident. At one of the evening sessions, he had told Elvis, Scotty and Bill to take a break. The three sat chatting and sipping Coke. Suddenly Elvis grabbed his guitar, banged on it and started singing 'That's All Right (Mama)'. He stood up and began jumping around the studio — just acting the fool. Caught by his mood, Scotty and Bill picked up their instruments and joined in. They were in the middle of the number when Phillips appeared at the door of the control booth.

"What the hell are you doing?"

"We don't know," said Scotty.

"Better find out fast — and don't lose that sound. Take it from the start again and we'll tape it."

Phillips was convinced this rhythm & blues song was one hundred per cent right as the A side of Elvis's disc. But this was a black song in the Deep South of America. He didn't want to offend white record buyers and disc jockeys and so he struck a balance by using one of Elvis's country efforts, 'Blue Moon Of Kentucky' for the B side.

Dewey Phillips was one of Memphis's top disc jockeys whose show ran from nine till midnight on Station WHBQ. The morning after Elvis had finished his disc, Sam took an acetate (a rough recording) to him and Dewey agreed to give it airplay that night.

Record Break

Sam got word to Elvis whose excitement was overwhelmed by his shyness. Telling his parents he was afraid people might laugh at the disc, he went that evening to the movies to watch *High Noon*.

He was startled from his enjoyment of the Gary Cooper classic by the sound of his father softly calling his name. Dimly he saw his parents standing in the aisle and slipped from his seat to join them. "Dewey Phillips wants to see you at the radio station," Vernon Presley whispered as they hurried out. "He says it's important."

'That's All Right' had made an explosive impact on Dewey's radio audience. During its instrumental break, he had told listeners this was a white boy singing and asked them to phone in their reactions. Quickly there came 47 requests for the disc to be played again — plus 14 telegrams asking when and where the disc would be on sale. Significantly, another local disc jockey had played 'Blue Moon Of Kentucky' on his

country music show that evening without any listener reaction.

Dewey had kept playing 'That's All Right' — telling listeners he was hoping to get Elvis in for an interview before the show ended. When Elvis — panting and nervous — came rushing into the studio, Dewey told him: "Sit down, please. When this record's finished, I'm going to interview you." Elvis replied: "Mr. Phillips, I don't know nothing about being interviewed." And Dewey retorted: "Just answer the questions and don't say nothing dirty."

Sexy Ways

Had he known in advance the sort of impact he was to make on audiences, it is possible Elvis might have held back. Or, at least, that his parents might have urged him to do so. For the young man who was raised along strictly moral principles was ironically destined to be the first rock sex symbol and figurehead for youth revolt. His mean, lip-sneering looks, his growling voice laden with sexual promise and, above all, his incredible pelvic gyrations were to delight kids and horrify authority. With all this going for him, he struck hard at the ears, the guts and the genitals of his audiences.

His first big appearance was on August 10, 1954 — shortly after the release of 'That's All Right'. It was an important country music show promoted by local agent Bob Neal and staged at the Overton Park Shell Auditorium in Memphis. Sam Phillips had talked Neal into giving Elvis a small, unbilled spot in the two performances and later Presley was to recall: "I was an extra singer in a big jamboree at an outdoor theater. It was my first big appearance in front of an audience and I was doing a fast-type tune that was on my first record and everyone was hollering and I didn't know what they were hollering at . . . everybody was screaming and everything. Then I came off stage and someone told me everybody was hollering because I was wiggling."

Twenty years later Elvis was still stressing his surprise when first he generated frenzy in an audience. "I really stumbled onto something . . . At the big auditorium in Memphis I was scared stiff, shaking and rattling all over. Everyone in the audience was hollering and shouting and generally going crazy and I didn't know why. I was dumbfounded. Kinda bewildered. It wasn't until I came off that I knew the reason. It was because I had been wriggling and shaking and writhing. So in my encore I wriggled and twisted more — and the more I did, the wilder the audience became."

Though Elvis had signed a contract with Sun, the firm wasn't in a position to pay a big advance on royalties and he even returned briefly to his job at Crown Electric. He was only able to quit when modestly-paid work in local clubs came in and when Sun began advancing small sums as the record's sales mounted. Gradually things started to happen.

Enjoying prominence because of 'That's All Right' and his Overton Park success, Elvis was given breaks in the autumn of 1954 on two top country radio shows: *Grand Ole Opry* and *Louisiana Hayride*.

His debut on the former was soured by the verdict of its head of talent that he should stick to truck driving. It is said Elvis cried on the journey home and was brought down for weeks. On *Hayride*, however, he was given a second booking and did well enough to be signed for a year of weekly appearances. For them, he had to get to Shreveport each weekend and this wasn't always easy because, billed as the 'Hillbilly Cat', he had embarked on a hard, far-flung, barnstorming tour headed by country star Hank Snow. Scotty Moore and Bill Black backed Elvis and at times they would drive night and day to make it to Shreveport in time for the broadcast.

Sam and Judd Phillips knew only too well that the youngster they had launched was becoming hot property. "The Presley family," recalled Judd, "were just nice home folks — very poor, living in a dilapidated tenement block. When we told them Elvis had a future in show business, they were real worried. Every day Mrs. Presley would call at our office with some new problem. She wanted to be sure we wouldn't be exploiting her boy's talents or overstraining him."

The Phillips brothers also realized increasingly that Sun Records — with its limited, regional organization — lacked the proper scope for handling Elvis in the likely event of his becoming a major star. And that's when the man who took Elvis Presley from being a small southern celebrity to rock's biggest ever solo star entered the story.

Above. Elvis at the start of his career, supported by Scotty Moore and Bill Black. Right: The power of the pelvis.

THE KING

Colonel Thomas Andrew Parker is still something of a mystery figure. It is said he was Dutch-born and christened André Van Kuyk. The "Colonel" is a non-military rank reputedly given him by the governors of Tennessee and Louisiana in appreciation of his drum-beating for them in political campaigns. When he came into Elvis's life, late in 1954, he was 45. An orphan, he had started work as a boy in an uncle's pony circus and had gone on to spend much of his life in circuses or carnivals.

He had often known poverty and he often talked about it: "I had this dancing chickens act. What made them dance? Well, *you* would dance if you were stood on a hot plate. But times were hard and often we'd start the week with six dancing

chickens but by Saturday we'd be down to *the* dancing chicken act!"

The Colonel first saw Elvis when the singer was performing at a cinema in Texarkana and was at once convinced Elvis had something. He knew showbiz — having promoted western movie star Tom Mix and managed such country singers as Gene Autry, Eddy Arnold and Hank Snow with whom he was now running an artists' agency. At that time — in the closing months of 1954 — Scotty Moore was managing Elvis on a friendly basis and on January 1, 1955, Elvis officially made Bob Neal his manager on a short-term deal.

The Colonel at the start was happy to act simply as the singer's agent and it was

he who booked Elvis for *Grand Ole Opry, Louisiana Hayride* and the long tour with Hank Snow. Moreover, Elvis's success in the *Hayride* radio series led to his appearing on the TV version of the show in March, 1955. Like the Phillips brothers, Neal knew his limits. Clearly, the fast-rising Elvis was going to need a manager with wider horizons. Equally clearly, Tom Parker was the man for the job.

For the greater part of 1955, Elvis's success was mainly confined to live shows and entries in the American country music charts. In the autumn came an appearance which was to have a vital outcome. It was at the yearly convention of the Country and Western Disc Jockeys' Association in Nashville, Tennessee, to which it was usual for record companies to send talent scouts. This year they did so with a special zeal because there was a slump in the record business and new performers who might boost it were much needed.

Among such visitors was Steve Sholes of RCA Records who had heard Elvis's first disc and kept track of his career. He now found Elvis had developed a powerful style of his own and his report to RCA was enthusiastic. There was also interest from other major companies and in the November the Colonel and Bob Neal went to New York to investigate the possibilities.

On November 20, 1955, Elvis's contract with Neal ended and he signed with the Colonel. Two days later, Parker fixed a deal between RCA and Sun in which the latter were paid $40,000 for Elvis's contract — a fantastic sum in those days for a performer who had yet to break nationally and which gave RCA the rights to the 16 Presley titles Sun had released and to a number of unissued tracks. Also, RCA paid Elvis $5000 as settlement of royalties which would have been due from Sun with which he bought his first Cadillac.

Those tracks were issued on an RCA album, 'The Sun Collection', in the UK in late 1975 and were: 'That's All Right (Mama)', 'Blue Moon Of Kentucky', 'I Don't Care If The Sun Don't Shine', 'Good Rockin' Tonight', 'Milkcow Blues Boogie', 'You're A Heartbreaker', 'I'm Left, You're Right, She's Gone', 'Baby, Let's Play House', 'Mystery Train', 'I Forgot To Remember To Forget', 'Tryin' To Get To You', 'Blue Moon', 'Just Because', 'I'll Never Let You Go' and two versions of 'I Love You Because' (both recorded on the same day).

Razzmatazz

The Colonel set about promoting Elvis with all his considerable energy, utilizing every bit of experience he had gained in the ballyhoo publicity world of the carnival. His efforts meshed powerfully with the vast resources of RCA and Elvis's phenomenal effect on audiences.

In a revealing interview, Elvis once traced his feverish, flamboyant performing style back to revivalist preachers he had heard in his youth: "I used to look at all those people singing. Real swell singers but not getting any response . . . kinda dead. But the preacher man . . . that fella cut up real rough all over the place — jumping, stomping, letting hell loose on the piano, bouncing one way and then letting rip in another direction. The congregation was rivetted. This was the difference between the preacher man and them good singers. I learned it was no good just to sing. You had to perform — give a show — grab an audience by the scruff of the neck. I owe my style and success to them church-going days."

Inevitably, and to the Colonel's relish, the press made much of Elvis's gathering reputation as a crowd-rouser. As one graphic report put it: "Elvis's drape jackets, pegged pants, and mop of brilliantined hair . . . His sideburns, boudoir eyes and his bumps and grinds . . . All these have an explosive effect on bobbysoxers."

It is said his first real fan riot was at a 1954 show in Jacksonville, Florida, when frenzied girls ripped at his white jacket, pink shirt and black pants and tore off his shoes. At the show was Johnny Tillotson — later to become popular for such hits as 'Poetry In Motion' and 'Send Me The Pillow You Dream On' — who said in a 1962 interview: "Elvis was in a country music package when I first met him and the show came to my home town — Jacksonville, Florida — where I was a disc jockey. This must have been right at the start of Presley's career because he had gone out with the package as first act on, but that arrangement hadn't lasted long because he had whipped up such riotous behavior among fans the show had almost been brought to a halt. So they had switched him to last act.

"I remember how he sat opposite me in his dressing room after one show — his eyes aglow, his hair wild and straggly and his body running with sweat. 'Gee,' he said, 'it's great, wonderful, fantastic — being in the center of all that noise and excitement.' Then he looked thoughtful and added, 'I wonder where it's all going to end'."

Vernon and Gladys Presley were only too well aware of what was happening and Elvis was anxious to reassure them. "Mom and Dad still haven't gotten over all this," he said at the time of his first headlines. "Mom hears me on the radio all day around the house and I tell her just not to get tired of it because that's a good sign. She and Dad used to come to all my shows within a hundred miles of Memphis but I didn't want them travelling further than that. In one way Mama can't take it very well. One time she was down in Florida when the girls began to mob me and she thought they were hurting me — pulling me apart or something. They were only tearing my clothes. I don't mind that a bit. I said, 'Mama, if you're gonna be like that, you better not come along, because this is going to keep right on happening — I hope!'"

Late in 1955, RCA released the first disc Elvis had made for them, the now legendary 'Heartbreak Hotel' backed with 'I Was The One'. Soon after, he sang it on his first national TV appearance — the show of top comedian/bandleader Jackie Gleason on which he shared billing with

Below: Elvis always ensured that he shared his success with his grateful parents.

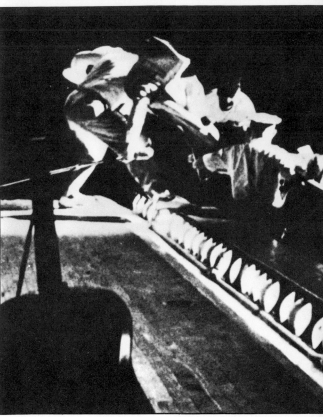

Stages in Elvis's first real fan riot at a 1954 show in Jacksonville, Florida, when frenzied girls ripped at his white jacket, pink sh

musicians Tommy and Jimmy Dorsey. He also appeared in a New York stage show with the Dorseys and within minutes of the start of his performance, the fans reacted so violently that fire hoses had to be turned on them, early manifestations of the incredible impact that Presley was to have on the teenagers of America and, later, the world.

Meantime sales of 'Heartbreak Hotel' were zooming and soon topped a million but along with the growing adulation and increasing success came knocks from the critics. One leading New York writer opined: ''Presley can't sing a lick and makes up for his vocal shortcomings with the weirdest and plainly planned suggestive animation just short of an aborigine's mating dance.'' Another declared: ''Popular music has been sinking for some years. Now it has reached its lowest depths in the grunt and groin antics of Elvis Presley.''

In Britain, where fans at first knew little or nothing about the Presley rock rampage, his disc sales started disastrously. Early in 1956, EMI Records — who had a release deal with RCA — put out 'Heartbreak Hotel' on their HMV label but for weeks — nothing. EMI weren't having this, nor were the BF Wood Music Co., who had the British publishing rights to 'Heartbreak Hotel'. Their chance came when Britain's mass circulation *Daily Mirror* splashed a full-page Presley feature by their Hollywood writer, Lionel Crane, on April 30. Headed ROCK AGE IDOL — THAT'S ELVIS, it began: ''I have just escaped from a hurricane called Elvis Presley,'' and went on to tell of fan mania at Presley gigs.

To ram home this formidable hype, EMI and the publishing firm took page

adverts in Britain's music press — plugging 'Heartbreak Hotel' and the follow-up, 'Blue Suede Shoes', and quoting from the *Daily Mirror* feature; ''What a frenzy this boy can stir up! I've never seen anything like it. When Elvis sings it isn't just a case of girls sighing and going swoony or stamping and shouting. I saw him send 5000 of them into a mass fit of screaming hysterics.'' A couple of weeks later, both discs were in Britain's Top 20.

Pelvic Thrusts

Meanwhile, RCA had brought Elvis to New York on a long visit and they and the Colonel encouraged him to spend a lot of time in Harlem's Apollo Theater learning what he could from the black R&B performers. Later there were reports that Elvis had cribbed the stage routines of some of them — particularly Bo Diddley — and in an interview just after Elvis's burst to fame, Bo was asked about this. ''If Presley copied me, I don't care,'' he said. ''More power to him. I'm not starving.''

Elvis had the power to create controversy. Nowhere was this more evident in 1956 than in his TV appearance. Ratings for the Dorsey show had shot up when he had been featured and the same happened soon after with Milton Berle's show. But there had also been a glut of complaints from viewers about Elvis's sex-charged convulsions. Steve Allen then asked Elvis to appear on his show with the proviso that he cool it. Elvis duly showed conventionally dressed and performed without his usual pelvic thrusts. Just the same, the show zoomed in the ratings and even topped Ed Sullivan's.

Sullivan had been king of the ratings and didn't like it. Briskly he declared: ''I wouldn't have Presley on my show at any price.'' However, the following week he signed Elvis for three shows for a total cost of $50,000 — the most he had ever paid an artist! His explanation of the action despite his previous promise was: ''He'll sing no suggestive lyrics for us. As for his gyrations, the whole thing can be controlled by camera shots.''

Sullivan kept the cameras to the top half of Elvis's body right enough, but the star gyrated his eyes instead — even appearing cross-eyed at one point — and the viewers loved it.

While his fame and fortune were growing, Elvis retired his father and bought his parents a fine house in Memphis. As he said not long after: ''I now had a way to repay my father and mother for the sacrifices they had made for me. In show business, life goes so fast that important things like remembering your parents can slip by. I made it a point not to let that happen.''

Indignation

But despite such noble sentiments, there was no end to Presley controversy. An effigy of him was hanged in Nashville and another burned in St. Louis; in the former city a disc jockey burned 600 Presley discs in a local park; the director of social services in San Diego said: ''We'll license Presley to perform here again only if he cleans up his act by taking out all those bumps and grinds,'' and the local chief of police added: ''If he does the same sort of show as before, I'll arrest

 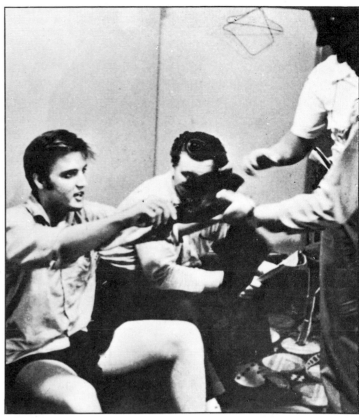

d black pants and even tore off his shoes. Such uninhibited behavior became a standard response to his sensuality.

him for disorderly conduct . . . I've had enough complaints from parents to assure me this guy is not doing the kids any good."

One critic jeered: "Presley's just a Jane Russell with sideburns;" another: "Presley offers proof positive that what burlesque needed all those years to keep itself free from expiring was a male strip-teaser;" but Walter Winchell, ace of the syndicated columnists and one of America's most powerful and feared newspapermen, opted *for* Elvis: "Presley has stolen the thunder from Johnnie Ray & co. He's the hottest thing yet to hit the teen-urge set."

Shrewd Colonel

Others agreed, including a professor at Arizona State College. He compared Elvis with the early Greek gods and said the Presley gyrations typified the origins of pagan ritual and that their counterpart had been fashioned by Greek sculptors. *Time* magazine found the spasms less graceful: "His body takes on a frantic quiver, as if he had swallowed a jack-hammer."

With Elvis, the Colonel's genius for publicity had come into its own. A Presley fan club secretary of the time recalled: "When Elvis came to town, we had to promise not to tell anyone. Then Colonel Parker would tip off the press and the kids would tear the place apart. Elvis would stay in a railroad car or in a trailer bus or at a motel. It was supposed to be a big secret, but later we'd find out the Colonel had leaked the news."

The Colonel organized fan clubs all over

the States and a flood of Presley gear which included 'I Love Elvis' badges for girls and 'I Hate Elvis' ones for jealous boyfriends! Meantime he was upping the ante for Presley's gigs — finally demanding and getting a percentage of the box office take. A spate of offers from abroad, being far below what the Colonel had in mind, were dismissed and it is alleged that a British promoter said: "For just one show, I'll pay you $300,000" — and that the Colonel replied: "$300,000 is OK for me. How much you gonna pay Elvis?"

When approached for Elvis to appear in the movie of *Bye, Bye Birdie* and to sing two songs, the Colonel asked $100,000. The shocked movie man told him such a sum just wasn't on. The Colonel helpfully offered: "Let's toss a coin. If you lose, you pay $200,000 for two songs. If you win, you get four songs for nothing!" Parker, of course, was playing from strength and was shrewd enough to know it.

The Silver Screen

Elvis *had* to go into movies — both for his sake and whoever was lucky enough to sign him. That person was seasoned producer Hal Wallis. But no matter how big a phenomenon Elvis might have been as a singer, Wallis — logically enough — wanted the precaution of a film test and so at his invitation, Elvis and Parker flew to Hollywood in April, 1956.

A studio official recalled not long after: "It's incredible! Presley has caused more fuss out here than Marilyn Monroe. Girls hang around in crowds and every day, more and more sackloads of Presley fan

mail are arriving and long-distance calls from all over the world are flooding our switchboards." It surprised nobody that the test *was* a success.

"It was quite extraordinary," said Wallis. "Elvis walked onto the set to do his test with a veteran actor named Frank Faylen. I hadn't a clue how he would cope, but after a few minutes I knew he was a natural. Like Sinatra and with just as much personality. He's going to be one of the biggest stars ever to come out of this place."

The test had assessed Presley's acting potential in a scene from *The Rainmaker* and his general on-screen charisma with a sequence in which he sang 'Blue Suede Shoes'. It triggered a deal starting with three films at $100,000, $150,000 and $200,000 each. The first was *Love Me Tender* made in the summer and fall of 1956 with Richard Egan and Debra Paget.

One top movie magazine reported Elvis's arrival for filming: "He kicked up as much of a storm as he had in less sophisticated communities. Hundreds of technicians, carpenters, extras, secretaries, wardrobe workers and friends of studio personnel milled about the young singer on the set — beseeching him for autographs and pictures. When he entered the studio canteen, important stars stood up to get a better look. Later his co-workers spoke highly of the polite, shy young man who addressed everyone as 'sir' or 'ma'am' and who never got on a first name basis even with those he saw daily."

Co-star Richard Egan remarked of Elvis: "That boy could charm the birds from the trees. He was so eager and humble, we went out of our way to help him." But

Tupelo, September 27, 1956. Elvis's home town turned out in force to see him perform at the Mississippi-Alabama state fair.

Love Me Tender: Elvis as Clint Reno (top left); on the set (top right); with co-stars Richard Egan and Debra Paget (above).

despite this and his own considerable fame it seems he was somewhat in awe of established movie stars. When told that Ernest Borgnine had warmly defended him as a performer, he promptly asked someone to take the actor a set of his recordings with his thanks. ''Be nice to take them in person, Elvis,'' was the reply.

''I couldn't do that,'' he explained. ''I'd get cold feet soon as I got to the door of his dressing room.''

Just in case he wasn't getting enough publicity elsewhere with filmmaking and discs, Elvis got into a fight with a Memphis filling station manager early in October, 1956. The story came out in court: Elvis had stopped his white Continental at the filling station and asked the manager, 42-year-old Ed Hopper, to check the tanks for leaks. Seeing the singer and the costly car, a crowd had gathered and Hopper had told Elvis to move on. According to a witness, he had shouted and slapped Elvis on the back of the head.

Elvis — all 171 lbs of him — then jumped out and punched Hopper with a right which gashed his left eye. Another garage hand joined in. Girls screamed and a cop intervened but not before Elvis had landed another on Hopper. When police asked his name, Elvis said; ''You could put me down as Carl Perkins.'' Hopper claimed he had tried being polite and had only shoved the singer when he started to get out of the car. Elvis insisted he had been hit first and said: ''I'll take ridicule and slander. But when a guy hits me, that's too much.''

Predictably, the courthouse was packed — mainly by teenagers wearing Elvis sweaters, badges and tokens, and cheers and screams could be heard from fans outside, all to the accompaniment of TV, press and newsreel cameras. When Elvis was cleared of assault, there was loud applause and Judge Sam Friedman thundered: ''This is a court of law, not a show.'' Later he snapped: ''I have never listened to rock & roll or heard Presley sing.''

Critics Sneer

A few months later Elvis received further publicity about a ''fight'' in Toledo, Ohio, but it was widely believed to have been a phoney — even though the star may well have been innocent of pretence. Louis Balint, a jobless sheet metal worker, took a swing at Elvis, saying his wife's ''insane love'' for the star had broken up their marriage.

Balint was fined for assault and then jailed because he couldn't pay. Later he claimed a Presley publicity minion had promised him $200 plus payment of any fine for pulling the stunt but that he hadn't received a cent. A Presley spokesman denied it all. It later came out that Balint's wife had left him long before and was living in Los Angeles, 2000 miles away. However, Balint had the last word: ''Know something funny? My wife can't stand Presley.''

More important in Presley's career was the release of *Love Me Tender* in 1956. It was the story of three men — the Reno brothers — who rob a train in the Civil War. It was not a musical — though Presley did sing in it — and its drama was heightened by the fact that Elvis was killed off. Although he was reportedly dissatisfied with his acting ability after seeing the first rushes, the public had no such doubts when they were presented with the finished movie. Indeed, it was said 20th Century Fox got their money back in the film's first three days of release. A measure of its impact on American youth was that when Elvis arrived in New York to promote it, fans massed round the hotel where he and the Colonel were staying — screaming protests about Elvis's death in the film and demanding a happy ending.

Love Me Tender was mauled by both American and British critics and in some

UPI/Popperfoto

The King in Court. Elvis, charged with assault tells of the scuffle at a Memphis garage in which he blacked Ed Hopper's eye.

cinemas in Britain, reaction was bad. The low was in Windsor, near London, where the film was taken off after half its scheduled run — the manager explaining: "Audiences were getting smaller and smaller and the booing louder and louder."

Despite this, Elvis's disc of 'Love Me Tender' sold a million *before* release and was to be iisted as his sixth gold disc with the flip, 'Any Way You Want Me', as his seventh. This was in succession to gold discs for 'Heartbreak Hotel', its flip 'I Was The One', 'I Want You, I Need You, I Love You', 'Don't Be Cruel' and 'Hound Dog'. The coupling of the last two had topped the US charts for 11 weeks — reportedly selling six million and in 1957 the golden lure of Presley discs went irresistibly on. His million sellers in the first part of that year being 'Too Much' and its flip, 'Playin' For Keeps', 'All Shook Up' and its flip, 'That's When Your Heartaches Begin', and the two coupled songs — 'Loving You' and 'Teddy Bear' — from his second movie.

Gracelands

Loving You featured Elvis as a country boy brought to the city and promoted as a singer by a smooth press agent (Lizabeth Scott) and contracted by a bandleader (Wendell Corey) and although some critics objected that the film didn't give Elvis enough chance to sing, it prospered at the box office. As he was obviously set for a long and successful movie career Elvis rented a house in Bel Air for a base when filming. What became much more famous was the 18-roomed, $100,000 house he bought in 1957 for himself and his parents. It was called Graceland and its address — 3764 Highway 51 South, Memphis — rapidly became well-known to all his fans. Consequently, soon after purchasing it he had electrically-controlled wrought iron gates decorated with two guitar-playing figures installed.

He was now established as a hugely successful international star and during his early fame, Elvis had made a triumphant return to Tupelo, scene of his boyhood poverty. As 20,000 fans at the County Fair screamed a welcome, he told them: "As a kid, I didn't have the quarter to get in here so I snuck in over the fence and usually I was escorted out. Now I'm escorted in."

He had been paid $10,000 for two shows, but when a few months later, the fair organizers had offered the same for his return, the Colonel said this was nothing like enough and had kept them in suspense about whether Elvis would appear till the spring. Then, unexpectedly, he had phoned the organizer to say that Elvis would appear for nothing. That second appearance raised money for the Elvis Presley Youth Centre — set in a park laid out on 15 acres behind the East Tupelo shack in which he had once lived.

It wasn't all unalloyed success though. A notable flop during Elvis's early career

A Presley press conference shows the intense interest he invariably aroused.

25

was in Las Vegas — scene of his triumphs many years later. The audiences at the New Frontier Club were hard-bitten and whereas teen fans had screamed their ecstasy at Elvis's singing and wriggling, these people mocked. But otherwise it was ceaseless triumph — with the Colonel masterminding everything with a sure touch.

It was reported that at one stage he was marketing 78 articles bearing Elvis's autograph and that he even charged for photographs of Elvis taken for publication. "A sure way to debase your merchandise," he said shrewdly, "is to give it away." When Elvis appeared at the vast Cotton Bowl in Dallas, the Colonel was seen at the main gate selling autographed pictures of him! When ribbed for this blatant commercialism, the Colonel countered: "Don't you never get so big you wouldn't sell good pictures for money." His hard-learned regard for money even led to charging writers and local dignitaries for Presley tickets and to renting war-surplus binoculars to back-seat customers at the big arenas where he played.

Uncle Sam

Elvis had been loaned to Paramount for *Loving You* and then to MGM for *Jailhouse Rock.* In the latter, Elvis was again a country-town lad but now the story was seamier and Elvis more of a rebel. In fact, he is in jail for manslaughter, and taught guitar by a cell-mate. After his release, he becomes a singing sensation and success goes to his head. Predictably, the film became one of America's top ten money makers of 1957.

Elvis had by now settled into his Bel Air house with an entourage of six Memphis buddies, two cousins, three musicians, three personal assistants and two secretaries. And his name was being linked with several Hollywood girls including Natalie Wood. He was starting to live the life of an immensely rich, hugely attractive young star. But his domestic peace was soon to be disturbed because, star or not, he was eligible for army service and just before New Year's Day, 1958, Presley, Elvis Aaron, was told to report to his local draft board for impending induction at Fort Chaffee, Arkansas, where recruits from his area were usually sent.

At this time, the film *King Creole* was already well into production and there would be vast losses in studio work and potential box office takings if it had to be scrapped. An appeal was lodged and an eight-week deferment was won.

The authorities hinted there would be no more favors, but this one brought numerous complaints to Milton Bowers, chairman of the Memphis recruiting board. Some because Elvis had been allowed the delay; others because he was being drafted at all. Amid the controversy Bowers said: "Elvis is a nice boy but we have drafted more important people. Take away his work as an entertainer, and what

Carefully groomed for Hollywood.

Left: romance rumors with Natalie Wood. Right: the supreme showman arrives for a performance wearing a sensational gold suit.

is left? Some nut even rang me the other night to complain we hadn't put Beethoven in the army! He might have felt we were discriminating against rock & roll, except Beethoven had been dead some time and wasn't even an American!"

Despite the protests, the film was finished in time. In it Elvis was again at odds with the law, this time playing his raunchy rock in a hoodlum's nightclub and the story — based on the Harold Robbins novel *A Stone For Danny Fisher* — gave him his best acting scope so far. Further-

more, Paramount had noted criticisms of his previous films and decided to work plenty of songs into the action — engaging no fewer than 15 composers.

While the studio pressed frantically on with the film, RCA were also hard at work. They had been preparing an 'Elvis Golden Album' to mark his induction. They also stockpiled Presley tracks so that they could issue new Presley discs throughout his service. Despite these steps it was going to be financially tough for the idol. It had been estimated that during the two years

service, he and the Colonel would have earned at least $5,000,000 but now royalties on records and films would bring only $2,000,000!

In truth, Elvis was set for life even if he hadn't sung another note. A deal had been made with RCA — mainly for tax reasons — for his royalties to be spread over 20 years and in addition there would be money from his music publishing and a cut of box office receipts from *Jailhouse Rock* and *King Creole*. Clearly, the Colonel would see all this income was shrewdly invested.

27

GI BLUES

The date of Elvis's induction in the army was March 24, 1958, but earlier he had to undergo a fitness test. As a celebrity, Elvis was given a solo army medical at the Kennedy Veterans' Hospital in Memphis. He arrived in a white Cadillac, wearing black slacks, black shirt, black waistband, black shoes and a crimson jacket trimmed with black! With him was blonde Las Vegas dancer Dotty Harmony, but he wouldn't be photographed with her, saying: "She has nothing to do with this."

He was passed A1 with above average mental marks, though a possible hitch came later, when a porcelain toothcap came loose, entered his lung and needed emergency surgery. Throughout the controversy and speculation surrounding

his call-up, the army insisted Elvis wouldn't get special treatment and he declared just as resolutely that he didn't want it. "I'm kinda proud about joining the army," he said. "It's a duty and I'm gonna do it. Dad's told me to be a good soldier or bust."

Early in 1958, plans for Elvis's induction and basic training involved relieving eight Public Information Office men of general military duties so they might concentrate on *the* event. Finishing work on *King Creole,* after the requested eight week deferment, Elvis was given a Hollywood send-off — receiving a Civil War musket and eating a slice of a cake bearing a figure of a GI peeling potatoes. He had a nine-day "last fling" in Memphis — renting

the local rollerskate rink for eight nights and reportedly having 12 lovely girls as house guests.

Monday, March 24, dawned cold and wet. Elvis reported at Local Board 86 at 6.35 am — 25 minutes early. With him was Judy Spreckles, blonde ex-wife of a sugar magnate who explained: "I'm like a sister to Elvis." Waiting were the draft board chairman and media men galore and, of course Tom Parker was also there — handing out balloons advertising *King Creole*!

Elvis was numbered US53310761 and made private-in-charge of the day's 14 recruits. They set out by bus for Fort Chaffee and after a meal at West Memphis and despite police efforts to stop them, fans ripped Elvis's civilian clothes and crushed him against the bus. At Fort Chaffee, a press headquarters had been set up, but these preparations triggered fierce protests. California's *Long Beach Press-Telegram* ranted: "A rubber-legged, hirsute, adenoidal guitar-twanger gets drafted into the service and, instead of letting him fade into well-deserved obscurity, the Army public relations officer takes special pains to assure full publicity."

Tragic News

Fort Hood's Second Armored Division had asked for some recruits with specific aptitudes for basic training and advanced tank instruction, and after three days at Chaffee Elvis went by bus to Fort Hood. "Presley was due about 4 pm," the information officer later recalled. "At 11 am, the media began arriving. I had never seen so many people at Fort Hood. We had cameras coming out of our ears." After a few hours of media pressure, Elvis at last got down to normal army business.

After eight weeks basic training, he was given the usual two-week leave. A girl in a convertible met him at 6 am outside Fort Hood and they drove to Graceland where his mother began feeding him well — hoping he would regain the 12 lbs lost in training. During that leave, Elvis again rented the rollerskate rink, recorded briefly in Nashville and added a bright red convertible to his car fleet.

Soldiers could usually get permission to sleep off-quarters if they had dependants living nearby. Elvis's parents were accepted as dependants, and he installed them first in a large trailer parked outside Fort Hood, then in a rented cottage in the area. But though he spent his nights "at home" he stuck diligently to army training. In tank gunnery, he came out third in his unit; he passed as marksman with the carbine and sharpshooter with the pistol, and near the end of advanced training, he did some duties as weapons instructor. His posting to Germany was not far off.

Elvis had hardly returned to Texas after his leave when there came stark warning of the tragedy which was to shatter his life. His mother was desperately ill and he and his father decided she must go back to Memphis to see the family doctor. Acute hepatitis was diagnosed, and Gladys Presley was taken to Memphis Methodist Hospital. Elvis was given compassionate leave and flew to Memphis.

Vernon Presley was given a small bed in the ward but two days after Elvis arrived, 42-year-old Gladys died of a heart attack. Elvis, called from Graceland, wept with his father at her bedside.

To Elvis, she had been not only mother but "my best girl." She had inspired his fight for fame and given him courage to cope with the pressures. She had fretted endlessly over his health, the mobbing,

Top: Elvis having taken his pre-induction medical leaves with Dotty Harmony. Right: in *King Creole* **with Paul Stewart who played a nightclub owner.**

his driving and the fusillades of criticism fired at him. Not long before her death she had movingly told an interviewer: "Even today he don't seem growed up to me. I still see that little tow-head riding the trike we gave him when he was three round and round the kitchen.

"Lots of parents don't let their children know when things are troubling them. I don't believe in that. Elvis would hear us worrying about our debts, being out of work and sickness and so on. He would say, 'Don't you worry none, when I grow up, I'm going to buy you a fine house and pay everything you owe at the grocery store and get two Cadillacs — one for you and Daddy and one for me.' Little as he was, the way he'd look up at me, holding onto my skirt — you know, I'd believe him."

Gladys Presley's body was moved to the music room at Graceland. Elvis wanted to throw open the grounds to visitors on the day of the funeral. "Mom loved my fans," he argued. "I want them to have a last look at her." But, advised by the Colonel, Elvis had second thoughts.

Marlon Brando, Cecil B. DeMille, the governor of Tennessee and thousands of others had sent messages of sympathy and 400 invited friends and relatives packed the funeral home. After a eulogy to Gladys Presley by the Rev. James E Hamill, the four Blackwood Brothers sang 'Rock Of Ages' and 'Precious Memories' which had been her favorite song. Outside, some 3000 mourners stood in tribute. With 65 policemen in attendance, the funeral procession made its way to Forest Hill cemetery, south of Memphis. As Elvis was helped by friends into a limousine after the burial, those around heard him cry: "Oh, God! Everything I had is gone."

Elvis stayed in Memphis another week, then returned to Fort Hood, to prepare for posting to Germany before embarking from the Brooklyn Navy Yard. On October 1, 1958, Elvis boarded the troopship *General Randall* and stood on the top deck — posing for pictures while an army band played Presley tunes. A press release had stated: "Private Presley showed outstanding leadership from the start and a fine attitude towards his service obligations."

Overseas Service

After the pictures, two of Elvis's training buddies were brought forward. Said one: "I think I'm talking for all the guys when I say we learned a lot about people in general when we were lucky enough to have Elvis with us . . . He gives so much of himself to those around him, you just can't help but improve a little through the association." Declared the other: "Things that would make the average guy as mad as a hatter, Elvis just took in his stride . . . You couldn't ask for a nicer guy as a great personality or just as a friend."

During 40 minutes of questioning by the press, Elvis explained that *Poems That Touch The Heart* — a book he was carrying — had been given to him by a friend and would be read on the voyage. What would

he do if his fans deserted him?

"I'd starve to death," said Elvis.

In Europe, what would he like to do?

"Meet Brigitte Bardot."

At Bremerhaven, German press and fans were massed, but the army had a troop train backed onto the local base and it quickly set off for Friedberg, 200 miles away, which was to be his permanent posting. The army struck a fair balance between military procedures and media demands. They declared the media would be admitted for three days, then the post would be closed to them, and there would be no visits to Elvis while he was on duty. "I expected a lot of kidding and embarrassment when I joined the Army," he told reporters. "I expected a hard time, but I have found that if I do the same things as the others, I win a lot of friends."

Duty Roster

The small town of Friedberg was delighted by its celebrated new resident. Elvis discs were played all the time in the town and shops sold masses of Presley souvenirs to the 18,000 inhabitants. The press had been told Elvis would be a scout jeep driver, but earlier it had been said he would be in the crew of a medium Patton tank. Explained an army spokesman: "The assignment of scout jeep driver is given to soldiers of above normal capability. The soldier must be able to work on his own, map-read and draw sketches, know tactics and recognize the enemy and enemy weapons."

Elvis's father arrived in Friedberg and took a hotel suite near the base. Soon after, Elvis's grandmother also joined him. She would be able to cook his beloved southern dishes, just as his mother had done. When Elvis moved in with them and began looking for a house, the Army insisted this was by the book: "Private Presley is being permitted to live off post under the military sponsoring act," said a statement. "What he rents is a private matter so long as he pays his rent and observes local rent laws."

After moving from one hotel to another, Elvis rented an imposing three-storey house in Bad Nauheim, a health resort near Friedberg. Around 10,000 letters a week flooded in for him — some addressed to General Presley — and to deal with urgent and personal mail, Elvis hired two local secretaries. But he also had his army duties to perform and he had been in Germany a few weeks when he went on manoeuvres with the 32nd Tank Battalion at Grafenwohr, near the Czech border. One of his jobs was driving a jeep with a master-sergeant as passenger, checking back roads because if his battalion were suddenly sent into action, fullest information about road conditions would be needed.

At Friedberg, on a typical day, Elvis would rise at 5.30am in order to report to his platoon sergeant at seven. He would then join others in his unit in mopping floors, cleaning and polishing, emptying garbage, washing windows and doing other chores. Then followed 15 minutes

physical training before going to the motor pool to check his jeep and clean it thoroughly. From nine to noon he would work on his training programme — studying such things as radio codes, communication procedures, range computations and map reading.

Afternoons were mostly spent in outdoor training and he would get home just after 5 pm for a meal cooked by his grandmother. Evenings were spent at the cinema, the local theater or in Frankfurt, 20 miles away. On Friday nights he would have dinner in the mess at 5 pm — then help clean up the entire post ready for Saturday morning inspection. On those nights he would sleep at the post — having attended the traditional GI party, where, if pressed, he would sing and play guitar.

"But," he said, "the guys mostly ask for old favorites like 'Danny Boy' and 'I'll Take You Home Again Kathleen'. They don't seem to want rock." A few weeks before Christmas, Elvis did what was probably the only paid singing during his service. RCA were given permission to

Elvis with his father Vernon outside the hospital room in which his mother died.

each number — going into the next almost immediately. He has a really fine voice — not quite Sinatra, but definitely Sinatra-ish — and is a very fine pianist indeed. I hadn't even known he played piano. Later I asked, 'You sing so well at the piano. So why bother with rock & roll in pictures and on discs?' He answered, 'I have a lot of fans who like me rocking. I like rocking too. So we have a good time. When they want me to sing softer ballads — I'm ready.'"

Certainly Elvis had come to terms well with his obligations to Uncle Sam. He had some sort of family life and a comfortable one at that. There was time and chance enough for wild oats and his name was linked with several German girls. But just the same, he didn't shirk his military duties. Had there been the least sign of his doing so, the press would have quickly given it space. He was diligent, maintained a friendly dignity and commanded respect.

Even so, the date March 5, 1960, can seldom have been far from Elvis's mind. That was when he was due for demob and others were well aware of that date — like the Colonel and Hal Wallis who had done a multi-picture deal. Also, the Colonel was planning a "welcome home" TV spectacular for Elvis — Frank Sinatra having been suggested as a co-star.

'Natural' Role

Hal Wallis certainly wasn't wasting time. In August, 1959, he began shooting Elvis's next movie — without the star. It was to be called *GI Blues* — a story with songs about US soldiers in Germany. The army had agreed to help and the Third Armored Division was used for background scenes. A stand-in was used for Elvis.

The star was by now talking often to Tom Parker on the transatlantic phone. They had to plan ahead because at the time there was much speculation that Elvis — coming up to 25 — might find the party was over and he and the Colonel realized they had to play their cards right.

Elvis, now promoted to Specialist Fourth Class, took his last leave in January, 1960. Once more he was lured by Paris and all sorts of stories about Elvis on the loose gushed from the press. One told of a lushly-built girl — rendered incognito by a leopard skin hood — dashing from Elvis's suite and heading at speed for the emergency exit. Elvis told the press: "In three days, I've had six hours sleep. I'll be glad to get back to the unit for some rest."

Shortly before demob, Elvis jotted down his conclusions on army life. They included: "The bullet-headed sergeant with the squawk-box voice must belong to the Hollywood army. I never met him. In his place I found a professional soldier — a hardworking, intelligent man.

"You learn a private has no privacy. In my barracks in Germany eight men had tape recorders, four had radios, half-a-

send a recording unit to the barracks and Elvis made an album for the Christmas market. The songs were in tribute to his mother and predictably, the album was a smash hit.

Sophisticated Singer

The following June, Elvis gave an unpaid, unrehearsed and unheralded performance which may be seen as highly significant in view of the way his career was to go after demob. He had 14 days leave and went to Paris with friends. They visited the Lido Club where George and Bert Bernard — brothers long noted in variety for burlesque miming to records — were appearing.

Later, George Bernard recalled: "Elvis came in several nights running and we got quite friendly. I was amazed at the boy, I had always thought of him as the complete end for the reason that I didn't dig his rock & roll, and his hip-swinging sickened me. Anyway, Presley was no score in my book — until I met him. Then I found a gentleman — as polite as you could ever wish to meet and as charming as a prince. After our second show one night, he said he'd wait till Bert and I had changed and then we'd go somewhere for a coffee. As I left my dressing room, I heard a piano playing softly, swingingly, soothingly, it reminded me of George Shearing. Then a voice started to sing, so quietly. It was a soft, bluesy number — 'Willow Weep For Me'. I *had* to see who was singing. I never expected it to be Elvis Presley — but it was!

"Surrounding him — some standing, some leaning on the piano, some sitting on the floor — were the waiters, cleaners, commissionaires, busboys and all the rest of the staff. But it wasn't the Elvis we knew on records. This was a suave, sophisticated singer at the piano — making magic at the keyboard — singing in a soft, well-modulated, superbly controlled voice.

"Elvis sang for about half an hour — a dreamy, contented expression on his face. He was enjoying himself. He nodded as his listeners applauded quietly at the end of

Above: the King's only visit to Britain, one hour between planes when returning from Germany. Top: Pte. Presley in training.

dozen had phonographs. On the dot of five, quitting time, all these machines started screaming out rock, jazz, classical all at once. Some of the men began singing, some whistling, some wrestling. That's army privacy!

"If I had only one piece of advice for a friend coming into the army, I'd say 'don't keep your troubles corked up. Work harder, talk to a good friend, learn to live with it. But don't jump into a mess you'll never be able to wipe out.'

"When a man goes AWOL, or gets himself into other trouble, most times it's because of a girl. If you feel you are losing your girl, don't make any fast, bad decisions. You won't get sympathy by wrecking a bar or stealing a car. Once you're written down as a troublemaker, you're stuck for life. You don't have to be a great soldier. If you just try — that's all the army likes to see."

Army Romance

The army, however, did Presley one favor. In 1973, Priscilla Beaulieu, the daughter of US Army Captain Joseph Beaulieu of Texas, recalled: "I remember that when my father told us he was being sent to Wiesbaden Air Base, I mentioned jokingly that Elvis Presley was stationed nearby and maybe we would get a chance to meet him. My mother said, 'I wouldn't let you walk across the street to see Elvis Presley.'"

Ten days after arriving in Germany, she was eating in a "little place where most of the army families went, when a guy asked if I wanted to meet Elvis Presley. I replied 'Fine' — thinking it was a joke. For my so-called date with Elvis, I didn't dress up because I still didn't believe it. Next thing I knew I was on my way to Elvis's house, which he shared with his father. Elvis was sitting when I arrived. He got up and shook my hand. Then reality hit me. I thought, 'What am I doing here?'"

Priscilla remembers her parents were still up when she arrived home — she was still only 16 — and told them Elvis had been nice and warm and cordial, but that she didn't expect they would meet again. Two days before he left Germany, he declared: "There is only one reason I am sorry to be leaving — Priscilla. Hardly anyone knows about her."

On the day of Elvis's return to the States — March 3, 1960 — Maguire air base had been hit by a blizzard and the wind swept icily across the base, pulling the temperature down to around 20 degrees below. Nevertheless at the airfield — near Fort Dix, New Jersey — a thin, freezing, straggling gaggle of girls had braved the elements to welcome back the recently-promoted Sergeant Presley.

Tom Parker stood in the enclosed reception centre counting the girls, and declared that the 46 who had braved the elements were equivalent to 200 on a normal day. The girls, though sparse in number attempted to make up for it in enthusiasm — pitting their screams against the wind, they slithered frantically forward as Elvis stepped from the plane. It made a stark contrast to the send-off in Germany.

The press conference at the Friedberg barracks had been described by a commentator as "a cross between a Hollywood premiere and an American government committee of investigation." Before the massed, milling media, the officer presiding had declaimed the official citation: "Distinguished, meritorious services . . . Initiative, drive, a cheerful performance of duty . . . Level-headed, even-tempered . . . Soldierly bearing . . ."

When asked about his future, Elvis replied: "I'd like to act a bit more in my movies. I want to do more serious stuff. After all, Sinatra has developed into a real good actor since he got that break in *From Here To Eternity*. I would like to try something like that."

He'd had trouble with his tonsils during his army spell which had led to speculation of undergoing surgery. He covered this by saying: "I've had trouble but I guess I won't have to have them out. If I do — who knows? — I might start singing real good."

As the laughter ebbed, he added: "And that would be real bad — for me!"

Meantime the screaming girls who had burst into the proceedings got out of control and Elvis had to be rushed to his car and as his motorcade sped to the airport it passed lines of sobbing girls. If Germany was sad to lose him, American youth was delighted to welcome him back.

As the press duly gathered at Maguire he faced another battery of questions: "Are you still going to make movements when you sing?"

Elvis grinned and said: "Sure. I just can't help it."

Someone asked about Priscilla Beaulieu.

"I'll stay a bachelor till I'm 30. Till then, there's room for everyone."

Vital Sessions

He was officially demobbed two days later — being given his last army pay and having already received a Certificate of Achievement for Faithful Performance of Duty. Inevitably, this was followed by more press conferences. In New York Elvis told reporters: "I don't know if I'll manage to get back to the top. I hear trends have changed, so it might be difficult. But I'm sure gonna try hard." However, he maintained that he would always stick to what he knew best: "My attitude to rock hasn't changed a bit. It would be a mistake for me to change my style. The public will let me know if they don't like it."

Below: Elvis as Tulsa McLean in *GI Blues*, capitalizing on his army experiences.

Paramount

Above: Sgt. Presley waves his military discharge papers and mustering-out pay. Right: with Juliet Prowse in *GI Blues*.

Elvis was due in Hollywood in a month, but before then he had to settle back at Graceland and cut much-needed new tracks for RCA. Back in Memphis he told fans and local friends who had gathered: "I'm mighty glad to be home — and to be finished with that old 5 am reveille. From now on, it's back to my night routine: bed at three, up at noon."

But there were changes in store because there was a house guest at Graceland — Davida (Dee) Elliott — a divorcee with three sons whose ex-husband was an army sergeant still serving in Germany. On April 12, 1960, Elvis's 44-year-old father announced that he and 31-year-old Dee were to marry.

It had been decided to hold the RCA sessions in nearby Nashville. Clearly, Elvis and RCA must have looked on them as vital because all through his army service there had been wide and prolonged press speculation about whether he would return to find his fans had deserted him. There were some ominous signs during the first part of his service. He had had a string of million sellers through discs RCA had stockpiled but then his sales had tapered off and he must have approached

his first session with some apprehension.

In the event, the fans gave their verdict *before* the release of Elvis's comeback single on April 1, 1960. It was a coupling of 'Stuck On You' and 'Fame And Fortune' and its advance orders were a phenomenal 1,275,077 — a world record at the time. It went on to top 2,000,000.

Welcome Home

But while his hit potential was the same as before, his home life was less unruffled. Almost certainly Elvis was restless at Graceland and although, reportedly, he got on well with Dee, his home must have seemed strange with his mother gone and the running of affairs in the hands of someone he had known but a short time. He left Graceland for Hollywood, where he was to start shooting *GI Blues* sooner than scheduled. Saying he had come to dislike planes, he took an overnight train — booking a luxury private coach for himself and his party of business associates, relatives and bodyguards.

His much-heralded "welcome home" TV spectacular which he had recorded in Miami with Sinatra, Bing Crosby, Sammy

Davis and other stars was screened six weeks after demob and had a mixed reception. Probably the most savage attack was in the *New York World-Telegram* whose critic wrote: "Didn't two years in the Army in Germany teach this twitching, pasty-faced lad anything? How to play the glockenspiel, perhaps? He looked awful beside the new, slick, assured Sinatra." But Elvis was paid $125,000 for his three songs and the Colonel announced any future TV appearances would cost $150,000 if Elvis happened to be available!

Vernon Presley and Dee wed early in June, 1960. Elvis couldn't attend because he was busy filming *GI Blues* at Paramount. Security was tight and he gave few press interviews, but it came out that he was finding it hard and was fluffing lines due to his nervousness. Despite any difficulties its star may have had, *GI Blues* was a box office hit. Moreover, the soundtrack album won a gold disc, as did the single of one of its songs — 'Wooden Heart' — which was adapted from an old German folk song by a writing team which included Bert Kaempfert. Elvis was still commandingly successful, still The King.

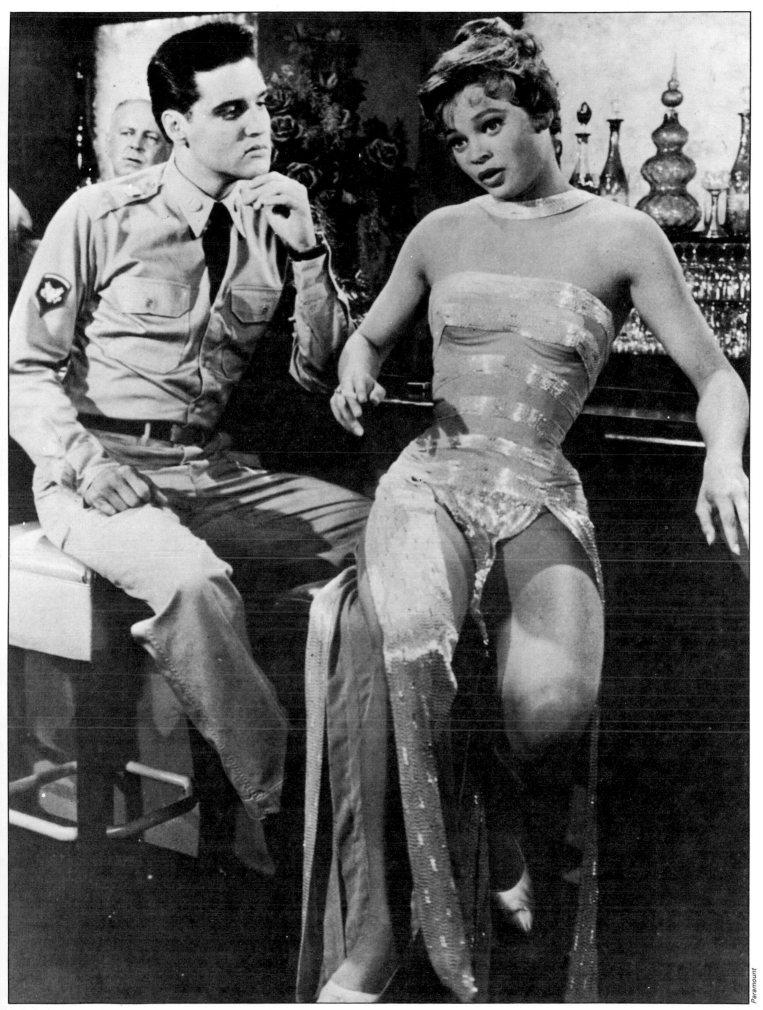

THE KING DETHRONED?

It was becoming apparent, however, that Elvis was changing his style. What was to be easily Elvis's biggest hit to date confirmed this. It was based on 'O Sole Mio' which had been written in Italy in 1901 and became a top favorite with operatic tenors. For Elvis, songwriters Aaron Schroeder and W. Gold wrote a new lyric and it emerged retitled as 'It's Now Or Never'. Although it was quite a startling departure from his heavy rock & roll style it rapidly became a hit and finally reached a fantastic sales figure estimated at 9,000,000, of which 5,000,000 sold in the US, 1,000,000 in Britain and the rest in Japan, Sweden, Australia, Norway and other countries.

After it had taken off, Elvis told an interviewer: '''O Sole Mio' has been one of my favorite songs for many years. I have often played the record by opera singer Jan Peerce and also like Tony Martin's version, 'There's No Tomorrow'. I had often sung the number and when I decided to record it, I asked the music company to· get a new set of lyrics. I don't read music but I know what I like. When a record date comes up I fool around with the number and have the chorus put in some 'oohs' here and some 'ahs' there and maybe add some piano and that's what I did with 'It's Now Or Never'. It wasn't rock & roll but it did have a little beat. I think it turned out pretty good.''

As a follow-up to *GI Blues*, Elvis undertook his first truly dramatic role in Hollywood for *Flaming Star*, the story of a half-breed ''torn between two loyalties, two loves and fighting to save them both.'' It had originally been written with Marlon Brando in mind and fans and critics were considerably taken aback when director Don Siegel announced he wouldn't be calling on Elvis to sing. As it turned out, Elvis rendered the title song plus 'A Cane And A High Starched Collar' but it remained essentially an acting role. However, it was hardly a film for his rock fans and many of them were to voice increasing disappointment as his post-army career developed.

Of the new film, Elvis told a reporter: ''I don't claim to know much about making movies. I leave the decisions to people

who do. As for the fact that the script of *Flaming Star* was written with Brando in mind, I'm glad they thought I could do a part designed for such a fine actor." Certainly Hal Wallis was more than satisfied with the way things were going with Presley movies. After *Flaming Star* he declared: "Before we start a picture, Elvis always listens to the score. Occasionally he will ask for small changes in the music. He has an uncanny sense of what is right or wrong for him and I have always relied on his judgement in our pictures together. We don't load Presley's films with social problems. Just pure entertainment. Making a picture with Elvis is the only sure thing I know in this business. I wish all my films made money the way his do."

It was estimated that Elvis's income for 1960 was over $2,500,000 mainly accruing from film and disc royalties. The only revenue from television had come from his spectacular with Sinatra, but the Colonel hadn't set an astronomical asking price just for the hell of it. "If fans are unable to see Elvis for free on television," he explained, "they are more likely to buy his records and go to his movies."

Left: with Dolores Del Rio in *Flaming Star*. Below: Elvis as Pacer.

Long-established singers like Sinatra and Crosby had been knocking rock and urging a return to the romantic ballads on which their own fame had been built. Elvis duly went along with that — with results which boosted his stock to even greater heights.

Many people had thought 'It's Now Or Never' his best disc to date and now he turned to another evergreen melody. 'Are You Lonesome Tonight' had been written in 1926 and recorded by Al Jolson and other stars. Elvis's 1960 version was untypical of his previous work, bordering, as it did, on the sentimental but nevertheless it achieved world sales of over 4,000,000 and in Britain it set a record for advance sales with orders of 335,000. To complete the story of his successful comeback and careful reworking of image it was announced at the end of 1960 that *GI Blues* would show a profit of $5,000,000, of which half would go to Elvis.

Romantic Bliss

In those days gossip writers were speculating that *the* girl in Elvis's life was actress Juliet Prowse. They were somewhat wide of the mark — though the truth about Elvis's romantic life wasn't to come out till a long time later. Contrary to her belief, after their first meeting, that she would never see Elvis again, Priscilla Beaulieu *had* gone on dates with Elvis in Germany. Her father was reluctant at first to let her go, because of her youth, but her mother had talked him round. ''Elvis was very down-to-earth,'' Priscilla later recalled. ''He made me comfortable, he wasn't aggressive with me and he never pushed. He was very gentle.''

When Elvis left Germany Priscilla again thought that the relationship was over and she was very surprised when Elvis asked her to spend the Christmas of 1960 at Graceland.

''I was dumbfounded,'' she recalls, ''both at the invitation and at Elvis's later request that I stay on. Of course, my parents said 'no' to that but Elvis called and talked to them and they agreed. It was arranged for me to finish my senior year at the Immaculate Conception High School in Memphis.''

Priscilla moved into the east wing of Graceland to be chaperoned by Vernon and Dee. At the time, she and Elvis didn't talk of marriage but she didn't feel awkward about the set-up. ''Elvis wouldn't have asked me to Graceland if there hadn't been a reason. I believed he cared for me and that he wouldn't have taken the responsibility of pulling me out of one school and putting me into another if he wasn't making some commitment. It was difficult for Elvis to buy for me, lots of times he would just tell me to get what I wanted, which I liked.''

Priscilla also recalled that Elvis would often rent a cinema where they would gather with friends. He loved action-packed movies including some Westerns and he · also had a special liking for Peter Sellers

in *A Shot In The Dark* but he *never* screened his own films. "He just preferred not to see them," she said. "Maybe he hadn't said a line right or thought his hair didn't look good or that he appeared fat. He just didn't want to see himself. He's very self-critical."

His Latest Flames?

Occasionally Priscilla would go to see Elvis in Hollywood but she was always kept well in the background. Meantime, the magazines were playing up alleged romances between Elvis and a number of girls. Dancer Dotty Harmony was quoted as saying: "Except it might have ruined his career, I'm sure Elvis and I would have married." Starlet Anita Wood was described as one of his closest friends and she often talked of Elvis and once reportedly revealed: "First time he took me home he just said, 'Goodnight. I'll call you.' But next time he gave me a goodnight kiss. How was it? Just like everything else he does — wonderful!" Elvis was even said to have dated a female wrestler called Penny Banner after seeing her beating four girls in a Memphis exhibition!

Juliet Prowse was supposedly the cause of a feud (real or imagined) between Elvis and Sinatra. The story was that Elvis, irked by having been outshone by Sinatra on the TV spectacular, hit back by taking Juliet (his co-star in *GI Blues*) for a weekend in Las Vegas. Juliet was said to be Sinatra's girl — and Sinatra at the time was said to be extremely angry and threatening what he would do to Elvis if he caught up with him.

But despite such "feuds" it was clear that Elvis's post-army image had been carefully planned. Gone was the riot-triggering rabble rouser who had outraged bishops and many others; in his place was the cleanly romantic entertainer to whom mothers the world over would give their seal of approval. Elvis had said, in Paris during his army service, that if his fans were to want ballads, he would gladly oblige. He and the Colonel now decided that the fans *did* want them and so Elvis sang them in films and on disc. The result was a phenomenal success — though it could possibly have been achieved had Elvis done rock versions of excerpts from the New York telephone directory!

Big Successes

His 1961 films were the dramatic *Wild In The Country* (in which he played a young Southerner on probation after running into trouble with his no-good brother) and the escapist *Blue Hawaii*. Both, inevitably, were box office smashes. And he had similar success with discs including million sales that year for 'Surrender' (a new version of the Italian evergreen 'Back To Sorrento'), 'I Feel So Bad', the double-A-side 'Little Sister' and 'His Latest Flame' and two songs from *Blue Hawaii* — 'Can't Help Falling In Love' and 'Rock-A-Hula Baby'. In addition, the *Blue Hawaii* soundtrack album became his fourth million-selling album. Released in October, 1961, it topped the album charts for 20 weeks in the States, was in the charts for a fantastic 18 months and had world sales of 2,000,000.

Money Matters

The next year, 1962, held similar triumphs with the movies *Follow That Dream, Kid Galahad* and *Girls, Girls, Girls* plus million-seller discs in 'Good Luck Charm', 'She's Not You' and 'Return To Sender'. So secure was his success that he didn't need television or live shows in the States, nor did he take any of the stratospheric offers to appear abroad. In Britain, for example, stories that Elvis was to perform in London were to become annual headlines. It was almost a yearly ritual that rumors leaked, fan excitement grew and denials were issued. Thus, early in 1963, one Samuel Areff was reported to have offered $700,000 for 25 Presley shows in Britain and the Colonel allegedly turned it down because "nothing had been said about transportation costs."

Left: with Tuesday Weld in *Wild In The Country*. Below: at the wedding of secretary, Pat Boyd and close friend Red West.

Left: a publicity holdup; Elvis and his manager, the legendary Col. Tom Parker.
Above: with Joan Blackman in *Kid Galahad,* the fight movie featuring Charles Bronson.

His earning power by now was so enormous that he must have been one of the world's richest men. It was estimated at the time that each Elvis movie cost between $1,000,000 and $2,000,000 and grossed over $6,000,000. There was also more coming in from "Elvis" products such as photographs, T shirts, rings, wallets, stationery and bracelets. These were handled by Television Personalities Inc. whose 1962 sales were put at $2,500,000 of which Elvis's cut was two and a half per cent. All sources were said to gross him an income estimated at $2,000,000 a year. Indeed, such was his work pace, he found just before Christmas, 1962, that he would be unable to meet a promise to star in a show for Memphis charities. Instead, he sent 50 checks for $1000 each — payable to the charities which had benefitted from his 1961 show.

With extreme wealth came problems — like knowing who his true friends were. Among his closest companions in those days were the Tennessee "gang." They comprised eight men Elvis had known from boyhood (including his cousin Gene Smith) plus Joe Esposito, whom he had met in the army. He surrounded himself with these trusted companions and they went everywhere with him — staying at the Bel Air mansion during his long periods in Hollywood. They each had specific duties and were paid but their general job was to protect Elvis's privacy and they rebuffed all questions about his character and way of life. In 1974 Elvis was to recall the parties he held in those days: "The boys would invite girls but I wouldn't have anyone with bad manners in my home; I wouldn't tolerate any swearing. There was always a lot of talking but everyone seemed to enjoy the healthy, clean fun."

Wholesome Image

At the same time, an alleged buddy of Elvis was quoted as saying, "We'd pick and choose the broads pretty carefully. We sort of shared them out and if any of the girls objected, she never got the chance to come again. The girls had to be impeccably mannered, that was rigidly laid down by Elvis. He might have half a dozen of them all around him on the sofa and he'd be leaning back, lapping it all up like a sultan in a harem. At midnight, Elvis would up and off to bed. I don't remember him ever going to bed with any of those party girls."

It's hard to believe that this white-washed image was close to the *real* Elvis Presley but, in those less enlightened times, the star had to be very careful what stories were circulated about his lifestyle.

For example, Priscilla Beaulieu might have been *the* girl in the star's life but it was kept absolutely secret. Today, of course, whether or not a star is living with someone matters as much to the public as which toothpaste he uses, but if Priscilla was his permanent house guest, the dent to his image — had this got out — could have been calamitous.

Elvis's "wholesome" way of life was crucial to his following. By 1963, even gossip writer Hedda Hopper — who had once clobbered Elvis as "a menace to society" — changed gear saying: "He's the best-mannered star in Hollywood and he's improved as a performer and has a determination to be a fine actor. He was smart enough to simmer down that torrid act of his."

Schmaltzy Sound

The gossip writers went on with guessing games about whom Elvis might marry and Elvis — Priscilla or no Priscilla — kept holding forth about himself and matrimony in the most general terms. Typically, he told a mass circulation magazine in 1963: "I want to get married and have children and all that. Maybe I could fall in love and marry some day soon but I'm not sure whether I've met the right girl or not. I've been working so hard, I haven't had time to get serious over a girl."

Hedda Hopper might have written of Elvis simmering down his act but at the time he didn't have an act because he wasn't doing any concerts at all. And, as for his style, he hadn't so much simmered it down as changed it altogether. His raw, fevered sound had given way to schmaltz and his singing in *It Happened At The World's Fair* which he started making early in 1963, continued his post-army easy listening, middle-of-the-road trend. All this was a long way from the potent sexuality and sheer rocking power that had made him a star and although many people thought he had sold out, "gone showbiz," and was a pale shadow of his former self, in money terms, it worked. At the end of that year, after Elvis had gone to make *Fun In Acapulco* and had gained three 1963 gold discs, RCA said he had to date sold 49,300,000 singles, over 11,000,000 albums and over 12,000,000 EP's. It was also estimated his movies had grossed around $75,000,000 and the Colonel declared Elvis had in 1963 drawn $1,500,000 in film salaries — with 50 per cent of the profits to come.

At the time, the Colonel talked at length to a US trade paper about his deal with Elvis. There was 75 per cent for Elvis, 25 per cent for himself — though on film revenues, the William Morris Agency took 10 per cent. He added that "at least 50 per cent" of his take went back into the business side of Operation Presley — which included office costs, advertising, exploitation and so on. "Elvis's take," he pointed out, "goes straight to the Memphis accountants."

Asked about rumors that Elvis's box office pull was being trimmed by over-exposure, the Colonel said: "Look — you got a product, you sell it. As long as the studios come up with the loot, we'll make the deal. They keep asking us to do more, so somebody must be making a buck. A producer was complaining that an Elvis picture of his hadn't done so well. All I can say is, he must like losing money. He's now after us for two more!"

Disc Decline

The Colonel's zeal for money was unflagging. Nor was it noticeably diluted by the urge — frequent in Hollywood — to get in the act artistically. Once a money deal had been made, the studio had full control of casting, script and production costs. "We don't have approval on scripts — only money," he said. "Anyway, what's Elvis need? A couple of songs, a little story and some nice people with him. Once we start telling people what to do, they blame us if the picture doesn't go. As it is, we both take bows and if it doesn't hit, maybe they take more blame than us. Anyway, what do I know about production?" One producer is alleged to have said: "I have a script which must surely get Elvis an Oscar. So how about taking a bit less than usual?" To which the Colonel replied with scything realism: "Pay us the usual fee — and when Elvis gets the Oscar, we'll give you your money back."

On the face of it, Elvis was riding as high as ever at the start of 1964 with films and discs, but a close look at his chart placings during 1963 shows that cracks were starting to appear in the Presley monolith. He is listed as having gained three gold discs that year for 'One Broken Heart For Sale', 'Devil In Disguise' and 'Bossa Nova Baby'. But these were for *world* sales. Judging by the US and British charts, they were not the super-colossal Presley smashes of the past. In the US 'One Broken Heart' from *It Happened At the World's Fair* reached no higher than no. 11. In Britain, it stopped at no. 8.

Possibly Elvis and all concerned had become worried about relying on film songs for his singles and a special session was held at the RCA studios in Nashville. From it came 'Devil In Disguise'. But on both sides of the Atlantic, its climb was steady rather than sensational, reaching no. 3 in the US while in Britain one music paper placed it at no. 1 for one week only. And 'Bossa Nova Baby' (from *Fun In Acapulco*), made no. 11 in the States, and no. 12 in Britain.

Maybe TV appearances would have helped, but Elvis still wasn't doing TV. In September, 1963, Britain's "Elvis Via Telstar League" urged the Colonel to let the star do a transatlantic show, but they had no luck.

Elvis's disc fortunes in 1964 were similar to those of the previous year. He had global million sellers with 'Viva Las Vegas', 'Kissin' Cousins' (both film songs)

Aspects of a long and successful movie career. Above: as Johnny Tyrone in *Harum Scarum*. Top left: *It Happened At The World's Fair*. Top right: with Ann-Margret in *Viva Las Vegas*. Bottom: the slick pin-up image (left) is reflected in *Double Trouble*.

and 'Ain't That Lovin' You Baby' — penned in 1958 by Clyde Otis and Ivory Joe Hunter. Most singers would have been glad of his sales, but they were modest in comparison with his own golden era. In movies, he was busy enough that year — with *Viva Las Vegas* (*Love In Las Vegas* in Britain), *Kissin' Cousins* and *Roustabout*, but none were vintage Presley and all showed signs that he was slipping into stereotyped plots which demanded very little of him as either a singer or actor. Perhaps it was all coming too easily, perhaps every one thought that having his name above the titles was enough to ensure a profit-making audience and so no-one bothered anymore. Whatever the cause, Presley movies were losing quality.

It has often been argued that Elvis's sales decline was due to his gutless, schmaltzy movie songs. Also, though the Beatles didn't cause the first falterings of his disc career, by 1964 when they conquered the States they could well have sped the decline. The speed and gamut of their rise to fame was totally unprecedented — outstripping even that of the early Elvis. Moreover, they had the added status of having songwriters of genius in Lennon and McCartney — whereas Elvis, though given writing credits on some discs, was on quote in the early '60s as saying he'd never written a song in his life.

Though the songs and the Beatles and the general coming to vogue of groups must have had a lot to do with it, it could be argued that Elvis's disc sales would have tapered off sooner or later solely because of the ebbs and flows of the record business. He could at any time have done live shows anywhere in the world for almost any figure the Colonel might have thought of and doubled, but he had done practically no live shows since his early days. Had he kept on doing them, he would probably have found — as Sinatra and others had found — that there comes a time when the screaming has to stop.

On the night of August 27, 1965, the Beatles came to Elvis. He had talked on the phone to Paul McCartney the previous summer and, according to the Colonel, had been eager to meet the world's most popular group. He had also been "thrilled" to get a wire from them congratulating him on his ten years in show business. But for months the meeting had been held up by the commitments of either side.

The Giants Meet

It did finally take place, however, amid great secrecy at Presley's Bel Air mansion. The Beatles stayed until 2 am and, according to reports, they got on famously with Elvis. They listened to records and played along with him when Elvis produced electric guitars and an electric bass which, he said, he was learning to play. The music was followed by much swapping of stories about life on the road. The story that Elvis wasn't doing live shows because he was too busy, was discounted by his statement to Lennon that his movie commitments occupied him for only about 100 days a year. When he added that a recent movie, which he wouldn't name, had taken only 15 days, Lennon quipped: "We've an hour to spare now. Let's make an epic."

But did Elvis like the Beatles as entertainers? In a rare statement on the subject, published in the autumn of 1965, he declared: "People have said my absence from personal appearances has given the Beatles their big opportunities. I know nothing about that. As for the Beatles, all I can say is — more power to them. I have watched all their television appearances over here. I don't think I should say what I feel about them. It

wouldn't be fair to fellow entertainers. I'll say the Beatles have got what it takes and in great abundance and that they've been given a heck of a vote of confidence. I'm sorry, but I have to be diplomatic and I'm honest about it. They are entertainers like myself and I guess they're as dedicated as the rest of us. Which, in the long run, is all that matters. I sure wish them luck."

That year Elvis had two global million sellers: 'Crying In The Chapel' (which he had recorded for an album in 1960 but not used on it) and the film song 'I'm Yours', which was listed as his 50th million seller. In movies, he made *Girl Happy* and *Tickle Me,* and signed a new contract with Hal Wallis. A Paramount statement said: "The money involved is around $10,000,000. If that isn't an all-time record contract fee, it is still fantastic money in anybody's language."

Defensive Colonel

Early in 1966, the Colonel explained Elvis was contracted to make three movies a year till 1969. "Elvis hasn't done a personal appearance for a very long time," he said. "We want to be fair to all his fans. If he appeared in Texas, it wouldn't be fair on fans in other parts of the world. Same if he only appeared in London. But his films can be seen by fans the world over."

Were his discs now going to be solely from movie soundtracks?

"Not strictly true," said the Colonel. "No film was connected with 'Crying In The Chapel' — his biggest hit last year. But we have decided to release only two albums and four singles by Elvis a year. His three films a year automatically give us enough material. Over-exposure is bad for any artist. Give a kid too much candy and he gets sick."

The Colonel then made the intriguing statement that 1965 had been Elvis's best year yet for disc sales — thanks considerably to continuing demand for earlier releases. Commenting on the decline in his chart successes, the Colonel said: "When Elvis first reached the top, there wasn't such a big market. Now in Britain alone he has to compete with 40 or 50 top groups. There's only so much money to be spent on records and so it's spread around."

Later that year, the Colonel was again defending Elvis — this time against attacks on his films: "People say Elvis's pictures aren't doing so good. I tell you we've made 22 pictures and 19 have been big box office successes, two haven't yet completed their runs and one hasn't yet been released. If his pictures aren't so successful, how come all the people who made 'em want him for more? *Paradise Hawaiian Style* hasn't finished 40 per cent of its run yet, but Hal Wallis called me this morning to say how happy he was with receipts and to discuss the next one."

Elvis with his highly experienced producer Hal Wallis on the set of *Roustabout*.

RETURN TO SPLENDOR

The knocking of Presley films and discs continued and one of the strongest attacks came from Tom Jones. Ignoring the ethic about one artist not criticizing another, the volatile Welsh singer slammed the Presley hit 'If Every Day Were Like Christmas' saying: ''I'm not too happy with anything Elvis records these days and this song just adds to the rubbish he's been doing lately. El is yesterday. His style of song has long since gone. Seeing as how he keeps himself so much to himself, maybe he doesn't know times have changed. He's certainly capable of singing better stuff but his ideas are so old-fashioned.

''When I was a kid I used to like Christmas songs like 'Rudolf The Red-Nosed

Reindeer', but these are surely just for kiddies. Pop singers should be able to get better material. In Elvis's case, of course, he either doesn't realize what rubbish he's doing or else he can't be bothered.''

Such knocks passed unnoticed and on April 30, 1967, the Colonel summoned close friends and business associates to meet him at Los Angeles airport. Among them was Sam Brosette, MGM's publicity man, who the Colonel had asked to bring ''two photographers who could be trusted.'' From Los Angeles, the party was flown to Las Vegas, checked in at a hotel and asked to be in the lobby at seven the next morning.

At 3 am, Elvis and Priscilla and four friends arrived in Las Vegas and drove to

the local Clark County courthouse where Elvis paid $15 for a marriage licence. They then drove to the Aladdin Hotel where Elvis and Priscilla retired to separate suites with their respective parents.

Brosette and the rest of his party were met at seven and taken to the Aladdin where media men had been arriving in droves. The Colonel had told them something big was cooking, but he hadn't said what. The mystery was dispelled shortly before the wedding ceremony where Elvis and Priscilla vowed to ''love honor, cherish and comfort.'' ''Obey'' was left out.

Years later, Priscilla was to recall how the decision to marry had come about. She had taken ''a good job in Hollywood as a model'' and had told Elvis if he wanted something, he would have to come to her. ''Although many people thought our wedding was sudden, Elvis and I had been talking about it in stages,'' she said. ''His proposal was without ceremony. One day he simply showed me the ring and asked me to marry him.''

Of the wedding, she remembered: ''Elvis put a three-carat diamond ring on my finger. The little diamonds went all the way round. With the Colonel's usual help and excellent organization, we gave a reception for the press and Elvis's business friends. Then El and I took the next plane to Palm Springs, where we spent the next four days in bed.'' The following February, a daughter – Lisa Marie – was born to Priscilla in a Memphis hospital.

To what extent, if any, Tom Jones's example inspired Elvis's return to TV and live performing, is a subject for conjecture, but the fact is that the Welshman had become an international sensation with a style of performing and methods of presentation very much akin to those which Elvis was to invoke with such fabulous success.

Mutual Admiration

One Saturday night in April, 1968, Elvis came to watch Jones at the Flamingo, Las Vegas, Priscilla and friends having travelled 400 miles from Los Angeles. They sat at a table right in front of the stage and Elvis could be seen joining excitedly in the applause for the Welsh-man's songs. During his act, Tom announced: ''We have in the audience a man I have admired for many years — Mr. Elvis Presley.''

Elvis and Priscilla went backstage to congratulate Tom and stayed for a long talk. Priscilla said how much she had loved the album 'Tom Jones Live At The Talk Of The Town', while Elvis said how great Tom's 'Delilah' had been. Elvis also recalled how he had ''died a terrible death'' in Las Vegas a decade before, and also revealed to Tom: ''When your 'Green Green Grass Of Home' was issued here, the boys and I were on the road in our mobile home. That record meant so much to us boys from Memphis, we just sat down and cried. Then we called the radio station and asked them to play the record

Below: the wedding in Las Vegas; Elvis with Priscilla, the girl who was his army sweetheart and long-time guest at Graceland.

again. They did — four times!''

Elvis and Tom had met only once before — having a short talk on the former's film set but after their Las Vegas meeting, they were to become close friends. At the time, Elvis had come right back onto the international chart scene with Jerry Reed's 'Guitar Man'. It was a powerful rocker — as was 'US Male' with which he successfully followed through and both seemed like a return to his former power. That spring, just after Elvis had finished filming *Live A Little, Love A Little*, it was announced he was to make his first TV appearance since the ''welcome home from the army'' one eight years before.

'Rock & Roll Lives'

During the taping of it, he told an interviewer: ''I'm doing this show before I get too old! There's been a big change in the music field since my last TV appearance. The sounds, the musicians, the engineers have all improved. Of course, a lot of the rock & roll today is basically just gospel and rhythm & blues — or it springs from them. Performers today have learned to trick things up with choruses and electronic gimmicks — but the beat is still there. It's still what I call rock & roll.''

Elvis was screened in December, 1968. Running for 50 minutes, it featured old favorites like 'Heartbreak Hotel', 'All Shook Up' and 'Hound Dog' plus several modern songs. It was a towering success which must have pointed the way with undeniable clarity to the next main chapter in the Presley career as his return as a live performer. But before that happened,

he made another long-delayed return — to the recording studios in Memphis. In January, 1969, he did his first sessions in the city since his departure from Sun 12 years before. From them came his biggest hit for a long time: 'In The Ghetto'.

Elvis's return to live performing was set for August, 1969, at the new International Hotel in Las Vegas where he was booked to do two shows a night for a month for a reported fee of $600,000. His last live show had been in Hawaii — for charity — in March, 1961, and his return was plugged ceaselessly on the media and in Vegas itself. Five thousand posters heralded his appearance and vast neon lights shouted ELVIS IS BACK and ELVIS IS HERE.

It was just the right set-up for the press to have got out the knives. Had Elvis faltered — had he failed appreciably to live up to his golden past and to all the razzmatazz surrounding his return, they would have killed him. But he was great and was acclaimed. One experienced critic wrote: ''For a full hour he worked and sweated, gyrated and shuddered, warbled and sang, grunted and groaned his way through 20 songs. It was a sensational comeback. Elvis remained the boy from the south — awkward, shy, full of evil promise and a dynamic performer. It is difficult to describe the exact appeal of the man. True, he is a great and rhythmic singer, but there's something more. His perfect looks and style add a charisma that is magnetic.''

Another said: ''Nightly he stalks the darkly red-lit stage . . . like a black panther who has escaped from his cage and has taken the first tracks back to the jungle where he was once king. The atmosphere

Below: Elvis and Priscilla with Tom Jones after one of his Las Vegas concerts. Right: the Presleys with Lisa Marie.

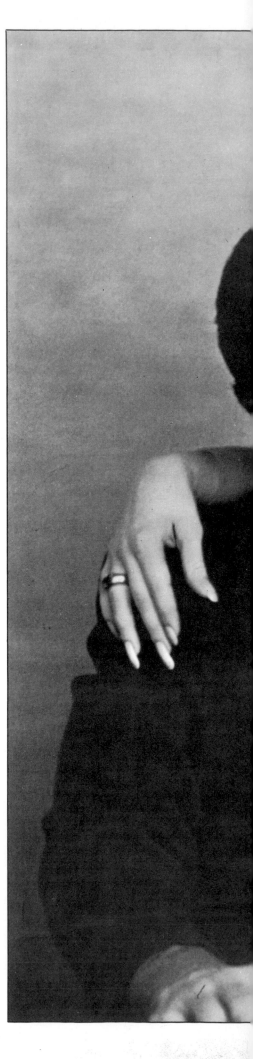

Elvis's dynamic comeback to live performances in the late '60s was indeed a return to splendor. The critics said his performance

is electrifying and Presley, a nervous gaze on his face, suddenly pounces. The nerves vanish instantly and the stage becomes a frenzied floor with Elvis the Pelvis back to a rejuvenated hip-swivelling gyration . . . The audience is ecstatic.'' There were many more such raves — some writers stressing not only Elvis's potent performance but his lean, youthful appearance.

During a press conference, Elvis said: ''For nearly nine years I've been wanting to perform on stage again and it's been building up inside of me since 1965 until the strain became intolerable. I got all het up about it and I don't think I could have left it much longer. I got more

pleasure out of performing to an audience like tonight than any of my film songs have given me.''

His act included 'Yesterday' and 'Hey Jude' — both Beatles songs — and he commented: ''I well remember my meeting with the Beatles and have recorded 'Hey Jude' for my next album. They are so interesting and experimental, but I liked them particularly when they used to sing, 'She Was Just Seventeen — You Know What I Mean!''

Elvis had been a sell-out in Las Vegas and a pointer towards his continuing on the live scene came when he did six shows at the vast Houston Astrodome in Texas,

drawing a record 200,000 crowd. There was fan hysteria in the city and in the Astrodome a police squad guarded the stage. The old days were certainly back and to enforce the fact he was back at the top of the charts in late '69 with 'Suspicious Minds' — a song that typified his new style.

In the early summer of 1970, the Colonel announced the master move that would enable him to capitalize to the full on Elvis's resurgence as a live performer and at the same time boost his foundering film career. It was to be a two-hour film documentary based on Elvis's concert and cabaret performances. ''There are a

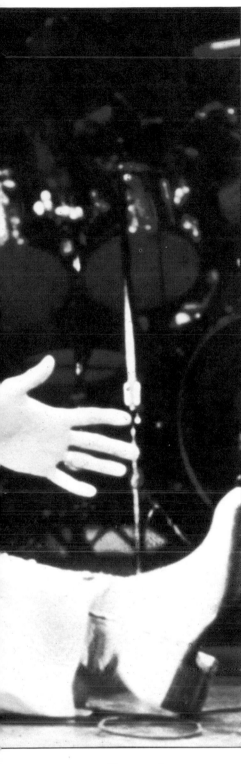

remained as magnificent as it ever was.

great many people in a great many places who don't get a chance to see Elvis's dynamic act,'' he stated, ''They can't all fly to Vegas so we're doing the next best thing and flying Elvis on film to them.''

The movie — Elvis's 32nd — was called *That's The Way It Is,* and was a mix of Elvis on stage, plus rehearsal scenes and shots of fan activitics. There were some intimate glimpses of the star behind the scenes including one sequence showing Elvis on opening night with a pile of telegrams.

The preview at Hollywood's Egyptian Theater was packed — though the only publicity had been a small ad in the local

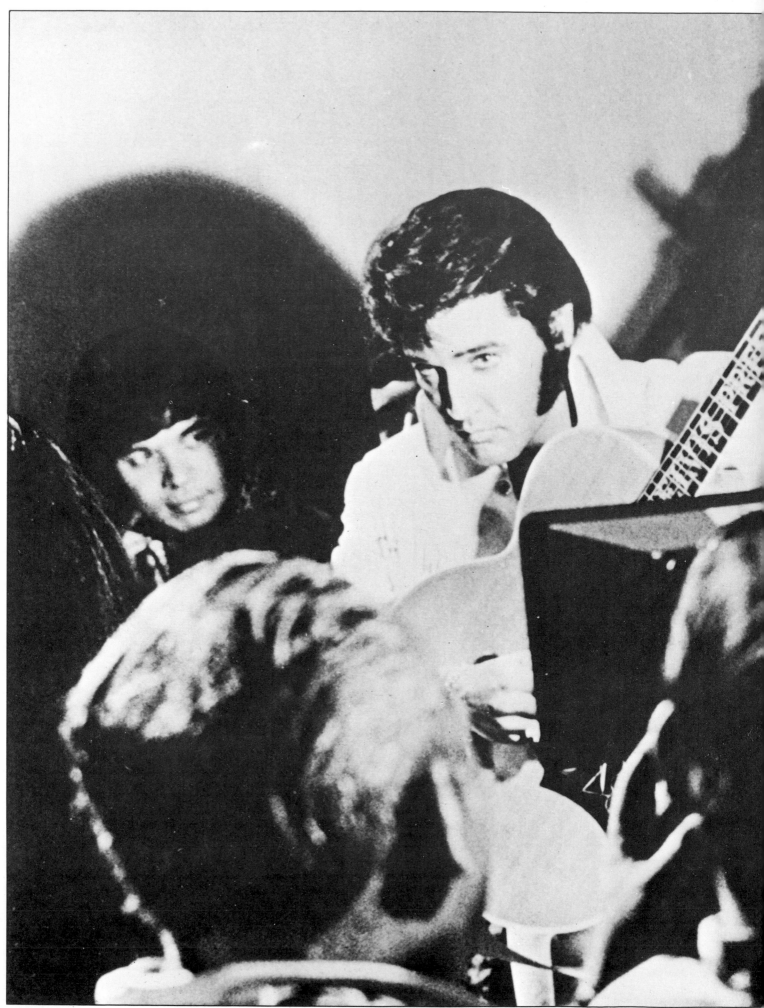

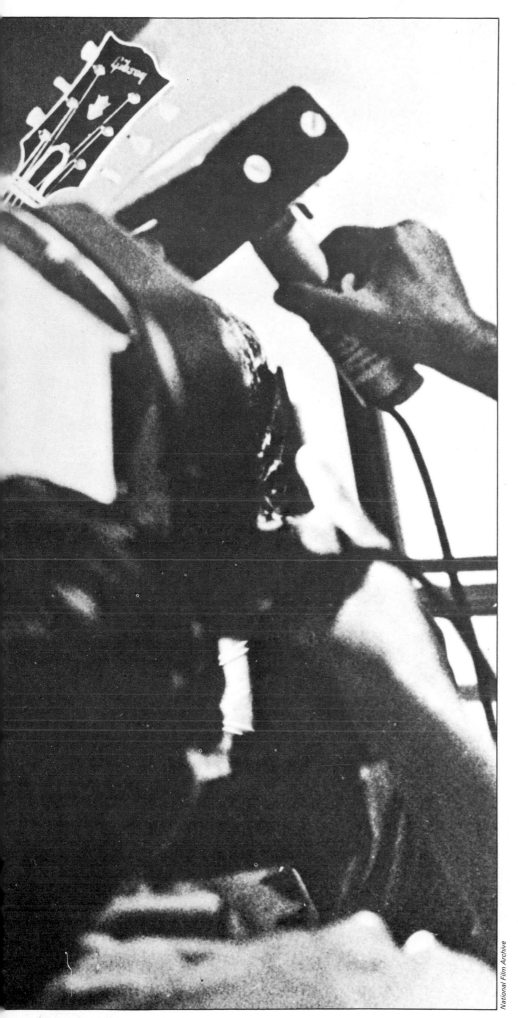

papers. It presaged the sort of attention the film would get globally because *That's The Way It Is* became an international box office smash in 1971 and his comeback was fully in orbit. His discs were smashes and he was in furious demand for cabaret and concerts.

In June the following year — after a one-nighter tour of the Mid-West and East Coast — Elvis played his first-ever concerts in New York, appearing before over 80,000 people at four shows at Madison Square Garden. According to one report: "The audience were not, as some had predicted, made up entirely of middle-aged people who had been 18 in 1956. There were plenty of teenagers there, finding out what it was we all used to rave about."

Satellite TV

Elvis held a 25-minute press conference during his visit in which he dodged political questions, saying: "I'm only an entertainer." However, he said he still enjoyed the stardom and wasn't in the least fed up with rock & roll. "My main trouble is finding good new songs," he told reporters. "I'd like to get some more material to record," he added, "but it's hard to find good hard rock & roll to record these days."

"What are you doing next?" asked a female reporter.

Elvis replied: "I'm going back to rehearse unless you got anything better in mind, honey."

RCA rushed out an album titled: 'Elvis As Recorded At Madison Square Garden' which had an advance order of 250,000 in the US and went on to become one of his top-selling albums. Another master stroke in his career came the following January when he did a one-hour concert, promoted by RCA Record Tours, in Hawaii. It was beamed by satellite to TV viewers throughout the Far East, and later telerecordings of it were shown in other parts of the world. In the second week of February, over one million copies of the double album 'Aloha From Hawaii Via Satellite' were released world-wide.

If Elvis had established a new chapter in his career, he had also invested himself with a new image. As a Hollywood magazine put it at the time: "In the early years, Elvis got burned by the country bumpkin label. The press seemed determined to make him look like Li'l Abner with money and he detested their efforts. Today, at 37, Elvis could give Mick Jagger a run for his money. For some reason he's dyed his hair even darker until it's blue-black. He's put rings on his fingers and bells on his boots. His suits are apt to be lapel-less — revealing a scarlet ruffled shirt with Napoleonic collar. His eyes are shaded by lavender wire-rim glasses with 'Elvis' engraved on each side.

"He leans on a walking stick with a

Elvis in *That's The Way It Is*, the movie that signposted the future for the King.

The King was overweight, but still high in popularity. This picture shows a posse of fans waiting to catch a glimpse of the star as he

silver bulldog's head — with diamonds for eyes — as a handle. Inside it is a gun. The corn-pone accent is gone. The country boy image has vanished. His manners remain. But there is a taunting, challenging look in his eyes.''

But while everything seemed to be hugely successful with his career, there were problems in his personal life and news reports in 1972 shocked his fans.

A break-up in Elvis's marriage was reported in July that year and there were no denials when it was said Priscilla had gone off with karate instructor Mike Stone who had gone to the Presley home at the start of the year to give Elvis and Priscilla

karate lessons and in August Elvis began divorce proceedings — on the grounds of ''irreconcilable differences.''

Rumors that Elvis might divorce had started back in 1969, after his Las Vegas comeback, his name during that period being linked with various beauties, and when the break-up was finally established, Priscilla declared the basic trouble had been Elvis's long absences, due to his work. With the divorce imminent, Elvis's lawyer declared: ''I'm sad to say the reason for the divorce is that Elvis has been spending six months a year on the road, which put a tremendous strain on the marriage.'' Elvis confirmed this, but

admitted there were other reasons. ''The problems,'' he said, ''have been building a long time. They probably started to brew when I was in Las Vegas.''

So, ironically, it was seen that the event which started his comeback was also the first cause of the breakdown of his domestic life. The divorce was made final in October, 1973, Priscilla was given custody of Lisa and there was a property and money settlement said to run into millions of dollars. By then, however, the girl in Elvis's life was said to be singer Bobbie Gentry.

Soon after his divorce, Elvis developed pneumonia and although he recovered

...ries out a new toy at Graceland.

and complicated by steroid injections and acupuncture treatment he had been receiving for a troublesome left arm. Other reports said he had an ulcer.

In March, he made his first public appearance for nearly six months — at the Las Vegas Hilton. PAUNCHY ELVIS MAKES THE FANS SAD read a press headline and the report went on to say he had a paunch and was clearly conscious of it and had told friends he needed to lose at least another 20 lbs. Photographers were barred and two who tried to sneak pictures were thrown out and had their films confiscated.

In May, one press report said: "Cocooned and protected by his 15 aides and body-guards, 40-year-old Presley lives the life of a virtual recluse. He sleeps till late afternoon most days and when he does awaken, rarely ventures out. He spends what is left of the day with his cronies and Linda Thompson."

Bigger And Better

In June, Elvis was in hospital for two days in Memphis, this time it was said he had eye trouble and was possibly suffering from glaucoma, a disease which could cause blindness. His personal doctor said Elvis had had iris inflammation for some time, that it had been worsened by stage lights and that he had been wearing dark glasses because of it.

In August, Elvis had to cancel a Las Vegas engagement after only three nights of a two-week booking. Again he was admitted to the Memphis hospital, and on discharge, he was said by the doctors to have had "a distended abdomen" and added it was not "caused by any weight problem." It was said he had been told to rest for three months and to cancel all engagements for a long time, but in December he returned to perform at the Las Vegas Hilton, doing only one show a night.

On New Year's Eve 1975 he sang before the biggest live audience of his career: 60,000 in Pontiac, Michigan. He made world headlines by splitting his pants! Two decades after he burst into the consciousness of a generation he was still able to outrage with his pelvic gyrations!

Into his forties Elvis continued to pull the sort of audience that stars many years his junior would have been grateful to have attracted. By any standard he was a superstar, one of the few personalities in rock music to equal the charisma of the Hollywood stars in their golden years. Elvis Presley was rock's first great sex symbol, the man who by his talent and personality had welded a generation together.

There are few people who can be instantly identified anywhere in the world by their surnames. Presley could. There are fewer still who can be automatically recognized by their christian names. Elvis could. Whatever way you look at it, Elvis Presley was one of the greatest stars of the twentieth century.

quickly, this was to be only the first of a series of illnesses. In August the following year, he had to miss two Las Vegas shows due to influenza. He returned full of fever and apologies — saying he had missed only five shows in 18 years.

Horror Shape

Elvis's girl at the time was said to be former beauty queen Linda Thompson, but one night he introduced his audience to Priscilla with the words: "I'd like you to meet my ex-wife Priscilla. I still love her very much — we just split up because I was away too much." In the November,

it was reported that Elvis had proposed remarriage to Priscilla — and had been turned down — and that this turn of events, plus a worsening of Elvis's performances, had led to strained relations between him and the Colonel.

Later that year, he had another bout of pneumonia. There were also reports that he was grossly overweight and had been dieting severely. In January, 1975 — around the time of his 40th birthday — he was again admitted to hospital. To avoid publicity, he was smuggled into a $400 a day suite at 4 am for a "routine examination." Some reports said he had a liver complaint caused by excess dieting

Death may have claimed him. The voice may be stilled. But he lives on as a legend. Millions of fans the world over were undoubtedly shocked by the news of his passing on August 16, 1977. But those close to him must have been increasingly concerned about his condition during the preceding months.

Early that year he took a car trip into Louisiana – only to cut it short because of illness. Back in Memphis he was again taken to hospital suffering from 'exhaustion'. His weight ballooned to almost 240 lbs – compared with the athletic 155 lbs of years before. In vain, doctors urged him to cut down on his compulsive eating – warning that it might kill him. Elvis didn't drink or smoke, but he was hooked on 'junk' foods. He ate doughnuts for late afternoon 'breakfast' – besides a massive dish of eggs and bacon. From then until his familiar bedtime of 4 am he would consume both meals and recurrent snacks. Favourite foods included hamburgers, creamed potatoes, pork chops with gravy, omelettes, ice cream and – above all – fried sandwiches of banana and peanut butter.

The medical diagnosis a few months before his death said Elvis had an enlarged colon and mild liver infection. Then there were repeated rumors that Elvis was on drugs. But they conflicted over whether they were being used medically to try and combat his illness or whether, as one writer put it, Elvis was "committing slow suicide."

It was also reported that Elvis was deeply depressed, not only by his weight and continuing eye trouble, but by the general advance of middle age and by his loss of sex appeal. For long periods he would lock himself away, talking to no one. Then not even Colonel Tom could rouse him from his deep apathy. Not long before his death his name was linked with lovely brunette Ginger Alden – 23-year-old beauty consultant. But it was rumored that he found it increasingly hard to keep her affections and was badly upset by this. Reportedly they often had rows in public and, in one of his tantrums, Elvis fired a shot gun into the air at his home.

Fight For Fitness

Despite his health, his appearance and problems with his voice, Elvis did not quit as a performer – even though his appearances became few. In late August, 1977 he was set for his first concert in the New York area. According to Linda Thompson, his most recent regular girlfriend, he had been working hard to get himself fit for this and for a tour.

It may have been his desperate fight for fitness which hastened his end. On that last fateful afternoon he was at his home playing racket ball (the American version of squash) with friends. It was violent exercise and the point came when Elvis –

breathing heavily and sweating profusely – said he must stop. He felt exhausted and would have to go to his bedroom to rest. When he had been gone an hour his friends grew uneasy. They went to his room and knocked. There was no reply. Finally road manager Joe Esposito broke open the door. Elvis was sprawled on the floor. There was no sign of life.

Frantically Joe tried to revive him, but there was no response and an ambulance was called. One from the local fire department rushed Elvis to the Baptist Hospital in Memphis. There his personal doctor and other medical men worked desperately to save him. But Elvis was gone. Said a hospital bulletin: "Mr Presley arrived in the emergency department at about 3 pm. The emergency resuscitation team began working with Mr Presley and continued their effort until approximately 3.30 pm, at which time Mr Presley's personal physician discontinued efforts." As the news sped round Memphis, crowds of fans – many of them weeping – began to gather at the hospital and around the Presley home. Soon police had to be called to hold them back.

Weeping Fans

Then, as the news spread across America and the rest of the world, countless switchboards in TV and radio stations and newspaper offices became jammed by callers unable to believe what had happened. Later it was stated that Elvis had been dead on arrival at the hospital and an autopsy confirmed the earlier report that he had suffered a heart-attack. Contrary to rumors, an autopsy finding was that there was "no evidence of excessive drug use."

Ironically some of the weeping fans outside his home declared that only a few hours before his death Elvis had come to the main gates, had smiled and waved to them and had seemed in fine health. Many of the waiting fans said they hoped for a glimpse of their idol's body. That many would get their wish was learnt when the funeral director announced that Elvis would "lie in state" for two hours on the Wednesday – the day after his death. Meanwhile, all over the world, TV stations were screening tributes and many of his discs were heard on radio.

After a private funeral at the Presley home, Elvis's body was taken to the mausoleum at Forest Hills where his mother lay buried. She also had died at 42. From stars and from millions of ordinary fans, there came a vast flood of tributes to the superstar who, for over two decades, had flourished in such unique and fantastic style. Two of the tributes possibly sum up the King best of all. Said Pat Boone: "There is no way to measure the impact he made or the void he has left." Declared Bing Crosby: "What he did was a part of history."

FILMING STAR

Presley, Elvis: Heavy-lidded American pop singer and guitarist, once known as 'the Pelvis' because of his swivel-hipped style. His popularity with teenagers survived a host of bad movies.

In this way was Elvis's screen career described in a weighty encyclopaedia of the screen. It may seem rather abrupt and even dismissive to Presley fans who have seen and enjoyed most of his 30-plus movies but is it actually untrue? Did he make a "host of bad movies"?

He certainly suffered a great deal of criticism and most rock and movie commentators do not think kindly of the period from *Girls! Girls! Girls!* in 1962 to *Change Of Habit* in 1969. In fact, one, Nik Cohn, has gone as far as to say (in his book *A WopBopaLooBopALopBamBoom*): "Most of his time was spent in churning out an endless succession of vapid and interchangeable musicals . . . and each one seemed flabbier than the one before . . . His voice seemed to have lost its edge and his songs were gormless, his scripts formulated, his films looked as though they'd been put together with two nails and a hammer." This is the sort of remark that makes his fans howl in protest and the British fan club — the biggest and most loyal in the world — has dubbed Presley critics "ogres" for their persistent sniping.

Money Movies

The truth is, however, that even Presley's most unquestioning admirer will admit that some of the films that rolled off the production line in his later Hollywood years were real stumers and few can find even the faintest words of praise for *Speedway* or *Charro*. In fact, the star himself is on record as saying about some of those turkeys: "We've made quite a few mistakes along the way. Mr. Hitchcock never seemed to be making my kind of movie, I guess." However, such flashes of candor are shortly followed with the shrewd analysis: "While I might not be too bright in choosing scripts, the Colonel's on the ball in fixing contracts." And therein lies one part of the Presley film philosophy: the films made money and so there was never any reason to break a financially successful formula.

In a way, Presley fans were *too* faithful over the years, too willing to accept indiscriminately everything that bore his name, too ready to rush to his defence at the slightest hint of criticism. From the very start the movies were tailor-made to suit the legion of fans. Their formula was simple but surefire: show Elvis as much, as often and as flatteringly as possible; keep the songs coming in regularly; bustle the story along as fast and as undemandingly as is consistent with skeletal plotting; provide a happy, romantic ending. The fact that the critics and the general cinema-going, record-buying public didn't much care for the films was completely irrelevant. They weren't designed for those people, they were made solely for Elvis-lovers and there were enough of them worldwide to show a handsome profit on a very low (for Hollywood) investment.

Celluloid Candyfloss

The fact that the fans asked so little of their idol on screen meant that he and his advisers felt they had to give little in the way of acting, plots, co-stars, supporting actors and, eventually, even songs. But criticism by most of the reviewers, at least in the early days, sprang more from sorrow than anger. They sensed, as others have since, that given the chance and the vehicle Elvis Presley could be a powerful screen presence and a film actor with the natural ease and magnetism of Frank Sinatra. The innate sexuality and energy that were conveyed so well in his concerts and records have never been adequately captured on film (outside documentaries) and many critics have been frustrated over the years by this wasted potential. The possibilities within Presley for memorable screen portrayals were frittered away on celluloid candyfloss.

To some extent the fans were to blame for this. When, for once, Presley was tempted into playing something different, dropping the songs-and-smiles formula and taking a hard crack at acting, as in *Flaming Star*, they didn't support him. Here was a determined attempt to fulfill the man's potential. He was given a first-rate director in Don Siegel (whose later work with Clint Eastwood in *Coogan's Bluff* and *Dirty Harry* showed how well he could handle stars who weren't great actors but had considerable screen charisma), a strong, meaty story and possibly the best supporting cast of his career. The part he played was not unlike that of the James Dean characters he so admired and he seized his chance to show his detractors a thing or two. And, to their credit, most of the critics acknowledged that he acquitted himself well. Judith Crist, doyenne of American reviewers, said of the film: "An earnest and restrained tale of misunderstanding and strife . . . a commendably unpretentious story." But she also pointed out, rather regretfully, that it "marked just about the end of Elvis Presley's foray into serious dramatic roles."

Why was this, even after the reviewers had made approving noises? Because, according to the Official Elvis Presley Fan Club, "for some unknown reason this movie has never been a very big success, box office-wise, with Elvis fans." It offers three possible explanations for this: 1. "Elvis only sang two songs"; 2. "The racial undertones were not very commercial although they were not overplayed"; 3. "The mere fact that Elvis fans saw only as much of Presley as they did of nearly every other actor in the film." To put it bluntly, *Flaming Star* broke the cosy formula that the fans liked and understood, that showed them their hero long and lingeringly, that asked little of their concentration or imagination, and they didn't like it.

Box-Office Champs

The proof of this love of the familiar format lies in the statistics for Presley's four most popular films. Every year the show business 'bible' — *Variety* — publishes its list of "All-Time Film Rental Champs"; this is a compilation of all films that have received $4,000,000 or more in rental to distributors from the US and Canada market only. It is an accurate gauge to a film's *general* popularity but it does not show how many tickets have been sold at box offices nor how much has been spent on them and it does not show how globally popular a film has been. In the updated tables published in January, 1976 four Presley films appear. They are, in descending order of receipts; *Viva Las Vegas* (429th out of nearly 700 listed; $5,152,000); *Blue Hawaii* (503rd; $4,700,000); *GI Blues* (577th; $4,300,000) and *Love Me Tender* (600th; $4,200,000).

That these should be Presley's most popular movies is significant: *Love Me Tender* was his first and therefore caused a great deal of interest and excitement; *GI Blues* was his first after a two year absence in the army and therefore also the cause of much excitement and a chance for his fans to reaffirm their continued loyalty. The other two, *Viva Las Vegas* (retitled *Love In Las Vegas* in Britain) and *Blue Hawaii* — first and second most popular respectively — share much in common. Both present Elvis as a happy-go-lucky, devil-may-care character who is attractive to girls, gets himself into lovable scrapes through unlikely misunderstandings but muddles along thanks to his charm, good luck and some quick thinking. Both are built entirely around Elvis and both are packed with songs — 27 between the two. They are prototype Presley movies, glossy and entertaining with high production values and good technical craftsmen both in front of and behind the cameras. If the Presley movie machine could have sustained the standards of these then no one would have complained as bitterly as they did about film after film.

Virile Action

The added shame of Presley's decline into mass production movies is that his screen career started so promisingly. *Love Me Tender* with its Western background and its solid support from Richard Egan and Debra Paget, who headed a strong cast, was the perfect debut for an inexperienced and obviously nervous young man. There was plenty of action to show him at his most virile, enough featured players so that he didn't have to shoulder the acting responsibility alone and even a few songs thoughtfully, and not too obtrusively, worked in to satisfy the clamor of his millions of fans. On the technical side he was supplied with an experienced and able crew headed by David Weisbart, a producer who had been responsible for James Dean's *Rebel Without A Cause* the year before — a fact that must have pleased Presley who admired Dean's work tremendously. The director — Robert Webb — had been a cameraman and, while not among the most creative of movie makers, had enough knowledge to elicit a promising performance from his unskilled star. This combination turned out an extraordinarily popular and, in retrospect, very decently-made movie that boded well for Presley's career in Hollywood.

His next three films continued the progress made and were all, if not Oscar nominees, soundly commercial and nothing to be ashamed of. All had good second rank actors and *King Creole* went one better by featuring Walter Matthau who was building up the reputation as a fine character actor that would one day lift him to stardom. This pre-army batch also included two movies produced by the man who had signed Elvis to a long-term contract and who was to be his major movie influence — Hal B Wallis. Over the years Presley worked for Wallis more than any

The changing face of Elvis as his personality developed from the raw early image to the smooth post-army days.

other producer and, as the man responsible for budgeting and overseeing all financial aspects of filming, it was he who dictated the sort of movies the star made.

Hal Wallis was one of the old-time Hollywood producers who had, in his time, overseen the production of scores, possibly hundreds, of movies. He had been a powerful figure at both Warners and Paramount before going independent and his list of credits is both long and impressive. He was born in 1898 and had worked in films since 1922, gaining, through his shrewd eye for a good story and adroitness at turning it into a carefully budgeted movie, a reputation as one of the most commercial producers in the business. Among the many excellent films to his credit were *Little Caesar, Casablanca, Gunfight At The OK Corral, Becket* and *True Grit* — all exceptionally entertaining and successful both critically and financially. Wallis brought this commercial acumen to bear on Presley movies and the two he produced before the army — *Loving You* and *King Creole* — show the care he took in building up his protege.

Powerful Sexuality

King Creole was a particularly interesting example; it is not surprising that it was reputed to be Presley's own favorite because it had a good cast and a fine director. Michael Curtiz was one of those astonishingly versatile men who seemed to be able to tackle any sort of film from a musical like *Night And Day* to a swashbuckling adventure like *Captain Blood*, from gangster movies like *Angels With Dirty Faces* to great weepies like *Casablanca* (for which he won an Oscar) and make a success of it. In *Creole* he had the basis of a Harold Robbins novel — *A Stone For Danny Fisher* — to work from and he managed to draw out of Elvis the essential power and sexuality, the rage and the pent-up emotion that came through in his singing and stage performances.

With this film; *Love Me Tender, Loving You* and *Jailhouse Rock* behind him Elvis, who had shot into the top ten box office stars in 1957, was looking set for movie superstardom when his call-up came. They ensured that his followers had something to remember him by while he was out of circulation and the numbers of them that clicked through the turnstiles to see *GI Blues* on his return seemed to indicate that he would fulfil the promise he had shown. *GI Blues* was a pleasant, not very taxing musical that showed its star and his beautiful leading lady — Juliet Prowse — at their amiable best. It was the first of many films he made under the direction of Norman Taurog, a very experienced movie maker who had come through the same school as Wallis. Born in 1899, Taurog had started as a child actor and been in Hollywood since its pioneering days in 1917. He became a steady, successful if rather unimaginative director and few among the many, many films he made in his long career stood out as exceptional. The best were *Skippy* (for which he won an

Oscar in 1931), *The Adventures Of Tom Sawyer* and *Boys' Town* which starred Spencer Tracy who was also reputed to be one of the actors Presley admired most. By the time he started working with Elvis, Taurog, like Wallis, was into his sixties and could not, therefore, be expected to be particularly sympathetic to, or understand the taste of the teen audience for whom he was making the films. It was inevitable, then, that he would rely on technique and well-tried formula rather than experiment with new ideas. And, while people paid to see the movies, there was no reason to change this policy.

The post-army films fell quite quickly into a routine and by the mid-'60s it was all so cut-and-dried that Elvis could admit that he had worked only 15 days on one of them. Looking at, for example, *Roustabout, Girl Happy, Tickle Me* or *Harum Scarum* (retitled *Harem Holiday* in Britain) this is not difficult to believe. It's interesting to compare the content and performance of these films — all made and issued between 1964 and '66 — with those of Presley's only real rock rivals at the time, the Beatles. Compared with *A Hard Day's Night* or *Help!* they look and sound old fashioned. They have none of the energy, inventiveness or fast-moving humor of the Beatles' features. That they were dated and out of touch with the tastes of modern youth was reflected in their relative financial returns. Both the Beatles' pictures took $6,000,000 in rentals according to *Variety*, nearly $1,000,000 apiece more than Presley's best, *Viva Las Vegas*. And while it is true that Presley appeared more often in the top money-makers, it must be remembered he made ten times more films. Furthermore, no Presley soundtrack score ever won an Oscar as did the Beatles in 1970 for Best Original Song Score for *Let It Be*.

Oscar Chance?

Does it matter, in the long run, how many times your films appear in the top lists or how many statuettes you win? Not when you and your backers are making millions, is the Colonel's answer. He once declared that money meant more to him than the chance of an Oscar and he was very protective of his and Elvis's investment over the years. This very conservatism may have held Presley back from the chance of trying something new. Perhaps it was true, as he said, that Alfred Hitchcock — or some equally distinguished director — never seemed to be making his kind of movie. But was he ever willing to try his hand at *their* kind of movies? The evidence points to the fact that he — or rather his advisers — were not. In 1976 it was reported that Elvis had received an offer to play the part of silent movie star and sex symbol Rudolph Valentino in a movie about his life and tragic death. Here was a chance to act a character completely removed from his own personality (although, judging from the stills from *Harum Scarum*, he had the looks, if not the proven ability,

to play Valentino's greatest role, *The Sheik*) and broaden his horizon. The Colonel turned it down when he learned that the movie would include mention of Valentino's alleged homosexuality; in the days of almost total screen permissiveness to decline on such grounds seemed unusually prim.

It seems strange too that, at the height of his fame when he could have been accepted by his fans in almost any part, he stuck mainly to nice-guy playboys or country lads whose background reflected his own. He tried three Westerns, two of which — *Love Me Tender* and *Flaming Star* — turned out well and showed he had a feel for them. (*Charro* was a disappointment despite an intriguing build up; perhaps in different hands it could have worked.) Surprisingly he never attempted that other favorite among singers-turned-actors — war films. The list is long — Sinatra won an Oscar for *From Here To Eternity* (and Presley is said to have admired his performance), Paul Anka in *The Longest Day*, John Leyton in *The Great Escape*, Bobby Darin in *Hell Is For Heroes*, even John Lennon in *How I Won The War* and others. It's not difficult to imagine Presley in such a vehicle but the nearest he got was to wear uniform in films like *GI Blues* and *Double Trouble* and neither was the sort of story which let slip the dogs of war.

Presley professed to enjoy movies as a way of relaxation. "I've always been turned on by watching movies," he once told an interviewer. "When I'm in Memphis, I hire one of the movie theaters from midnight several times a week and invite anyone who's around to see them with me. I love '30s musicals and gangster pictures." He reportedly admired the acting of Marlon Brando and hero-

worshipped James Dean and it's odd that this enthusiasm for watching films and observing fine acting did not fire him with a desire to stretch himself. Possibly his ambitions expressed around the time of *King Creole,* when he said he was delighted to be playing someone other than himself, were soon crushed by his fans' lack of acceptance and just because it was easier, twice a year, to stroll through a daft script than fight for something better.

Simpering Starlets

The pity of it is that Elvis Presley had the looks, the charisma, the voice and probably the talent to become a very popular, very successful and possibly very good screen actor. Somewhere along the way he threw it all away and settled for singing silly songs like 'There's No Room To Rhumba In A Sports Car', surrounded by simpering anonymous starlets in tissue-thin plots that demanded no more of him than an ability to smile, clinch and throw a punch.

That being said, no one can ignore the fact — mainly because the Colonel would never let them! — that Presley was the only rock star to have made a lengthy career for himself in movies. His films have probably made, globally, more money than those of most stars with careers twice as long. They have given millions of people many hours of harmless, happy enjoyment and will go on doing so as they are screened on TV. From the very start Presley films regularly and consistently did exactly what they were always intended to do — appeal to his fans. Elvis Presley never became a huge international screen actor who appealed to fans, critics and the general public alike simply because he never wanted to and he never needed to.

Popperfoto

REEL BY REEL

LOVE ME TENDER (1956)
20th Century Fox

Vance	*Richard Egan*
Cathy	*Debra Paget*
Clint	*Elvis*
Producer	*David Weisbart*
Director	*Robert D Webb*

Songs   Love Me Tender; Poor Boy; We're Gonna Move; Let Me

Synopsis   The Reno brothers — Vance, Brett and Ray — are Confederate marauders in the Civil War whose last raid on a Federal payroll is unwittingly staged after the South has surrendered. Having split the proceeds with their colleagues they return home to find that their younger brother, Clint, has married Vance's fiancee, Cathy, under the mistaken belief that he is dead.

The difficult situation is made worse by the arrival of a posse that arrests the three Renos for robbery. Clint, believing them to be innocent, stages a rescue and is astonished when Vance orders the loot to be handed over to the authorities. The brothers' share is on the farm and by a tragic misunderstanding Clint believes that Cathy and Vance have double-crossed him and run off together with the money. Unhinged by the sequence of events he shoots Vance and is in turn fatally shot.

Reviews

"Thick-lipped, droopy-eyed, and indefatigably sullen, Mr. Presley, whose talents are meager . . . excites a large section of the young female population . . . and I approached his movie with a certain amount of middle-aged trepidation. Unhappily, my fears were well founded," said John McCarten of the *New Yorker* and echoed the thoughts of many cynical critics. "If Elvis had not sung his four fabulous numbers then he would have been an absolute flop filmwise . . ." opined a fan club correspondent who concluded that "considering the weak story, the small, totally unsuitable role and the almost childlike persistence of the other stars in trying to 'better' Elvis's lines — Elvis came out tops."

LOVING YOU (1957)
Paramount

Deke Rivers	*Elvis*
Glenda Markle	*Lizabeth Scott*
Walter 'Tex' Warner	*Wendell Corey*
Carl	*James Gleason*
Producer	*Hal Wallis*
Director	*Hal Kanter*

Songs Lonesome Cowboy; Party; Teddy Bear; Hot Dog; Got A Lot A Livin' To Do; Mean Woman Blues; Loving You; Candy Kisses

Synopsis A smart press agent, Glenda Markle, spots the potential of young Deke when she sees him at a show given by her unsuccessful ex-husband's band. Having seen the galvanic effect his singing has on audiences, she realizes that he could take Tex's band back into the bigtime. As she works to increase Deke's success he becomes increasingly bewildered by his fame and the outrage to parents and hysteria among teens that his performances cause. Glenda manipulates him against his will to further popularity and notoriety by any means she can, including allowing him to believe she's fallen in love with him. Learning the truth of the matter he drives off just before he's due to star in a TV spectacular and only a last minute intervention brings him back to acclaim and superstardom.

Reviews This movie, which was obviously based on Elvis's own meteoric rise, was generally well received and gained acclaim as "a perfect Presley vehicle" with comments on the charm of "the star's deadpan performance with the swivel of hip, dangle of forelock and tremble of baritone to convey the hungers of a lonely soul."

JAILHOUSE ROCK *(1957)*
M.G.M.

Vince Everett	*Elvis*
Peggy Van Alden	*Judy Tyler*
Hunk Houghton	*Mickey Shaughnessy*
Sherry Wilson	*Jennifer Holden*
Teddy Talbot	*Dean Jones*
Producer	*Pandro S Berman*
Director	*Richard Thorpe*

Songs Jailhouse Rock; Treat Me Nice; Young And Beautiful; I Wanna Be Free; Don't Leave Me Now; Baby I Don't Care; One More Day (sung by Shaughnessy)

Synopsis Vince Everett is sentenced to prison for manslaughter after accidentally killing a man. Inside he meets Hunk Houghton who spots his musical talents and encourages him to sing. They decide to form a partnership as a duo when they get out but Vince, who is released first, is discovered by a talent scout, Peggy Van Alden, and by the time Hunk is freed, Vince is a big solo star. Fame turns Vince's head and blinds him to the love of Peggy and friendship of Hunk until his high-handed behavior results in a fight between the two ex-buddies in the course of which he receives a career-threatening blow in the throat. Helped by Peggy's love and the now-contrite Hunk, Vince is nursed back to money-spinning health.

Reviews Generally liked for its verve and, of course, a favorite classic to all Presley and most rock fans, the critics have accorded Elvis grudging respect over the years with comments like "he shivers and shakes with gusto, much more than is provided by the script" and "despite the lamentable title, this isn't at all a bad Elvis Presley vehicle."

KING CREOLE *(1958)*
Paramount

Danny Fisher	*Elvis*
Ronnie	*Carolyn Jones*
Nellie	*Dolores Hart*
Mr. Fisher	*Dean Jagger*
Maxie Fields	*Walter Matthau*
Producer	*Hal Wallis*
Director	*Michael Curtiz*
	Based on Harold Robbins's *A Stone For Danny Fisher*

Songs As Long As I Have You; Crawfish; King Creole; Don't Ask Me Why; New Orleans; Lover Doll; Hard-Headed Woman; Trouble; Steadfast, Loyal And True; Young Dreams; Dixieland Rock; Banana (sung by Lilliane Montevecchi)

Synopsis Danny Fisher, under pressure from his father to do well at school and the need to earn a living, is tempted towards a life of crime in the violent underworld of New Orleans. He takes part in a successful shoplifting raid but is persuaded by Nellie to abandon crime even though the club where he works nights is owned by a vicious gangster, Maxie Fields. A rival club owner recognizes Danny's performing talent and signs him to star with the result that Fields's club loses customers; in an attempt to get Danny into his clutches Fields orders a henchman to involve Danny in a crime and he is lured into an attack on his father's employer. By mistake it is Mr. Fisher who gets beaten before Danny arrives to help and he is hospitalized at Fields's expense, who consequently has Danny indebted to him. He seeks repayment by having the boy work in his club and maliciously tells Mr. Fisher that Danny helped to beat him up. Danny seeks revenge, has a successful showdown with Fields, is reconciled with his father and united with Nellie.

Reviews Elvis relished this part and said: "For the first time in my screen career, I'm playing someone other than Elvis Presley." It is said to be his own favorite film and is generally well-considered although one magazine described it as "the most unattractive Presley vehicle so far." However, a British critic, Elkan Allan, has declared: "His best film . . . if he had taken this as the starting-point for a serious career he might really have achieved something."

GI BLUES *(1960)*

Paramount

Tulsa McLean	*Elvis*
Lili	*Juliet Prowse*
Cooky	*Robert Ivers*
Tina	*Leticia Roman*
Producer	*Hal Wallis*
Director	*Norman Taurog*

Songs GI Blues; Blue Suede Shoes; Tonight Is So Right For Love; Frankfurt Special; Wooden Heart; Pocketful Of Rainbows; Didja Ever?; What's She Really Like?; Shoppin' Around; Big Boots; Doin' The Best I Can

Synopsis Tulsa McLean and two GI buddies play in a group and plan to open a nightclub when they are demobbed. To win a bet Tulsa undertakes to spend a night with Lili, a popular dancer with an iceberg reputation. Under the intense but covert scrutiny of the gamblers he meets and charms Lili and they do spend the night together — innocently babysitting! The bet is won, the money safe but Lili misunderstands Tulsa's intentions, thinking he only wants her as a money-object. Eventually, however, the muddle is sorted out and love declared.

Reviews The film had a better than average score and helped confirm Elvis's continued popularity despite an enforced absence. Most critics agreed that it was "a pleasant Presley musical that should satisfy his fans, while others should find some fun along the way," but one critic felt that Juliet Prowse deserved a leading man "with more genuine fire. than Presley." The film's popularity is confirmed by its position in the 1976 *Variety* list of "All-Time Film Rental Champs" where it stood at position 577 with US/Canada rental receipts of $4,300,000.

FLAMING STAR *(1960)*

20th Century Fox

Pacer	*Elvis*
Roslyn Pierce	*Barbara Eden*
Clint	*Steve Forrest*
Neddy Burton	*Dolores Del Rio*
Pa Burton	*John McIntire*
Producer	*David Weisbart*
Director	*Don Siegel*

Songs Flaming Star; A Cane And A High Starched Collar

Synopsis This movie has one of the strongest support casts that ever surrounded Elvis and certainly one of the best directors in Don Siegel who went on to work extensively with Clint Eastwood and made such films as *Coogan's Bluff, Dirty Harry* and *Charley Varrick*. The story centers around the problems faced by Pacer who is the half-breed son of a white father and Kiowa Indian mother. Following the massacre of a family, Pacer, his parents and brother Clint find themselves caught between two cultures. Pacer is accused by the towns-people of complicity and, following his father's refusal to join a reprisal raid, Clint shoots one of its members who insults his mother. The Kiowas want Pacer to join them and his mother tries to parley peace but is seriously wounded in a tragic misunderstanding. The townsfolk refuse the family medical assistance until Clint and Pacer hold a child hostage but by the time the doctor arrives their mother is dead and Pacer turns his back on whites. Brother is set against brother until their father becomes a victim and despite severe injuries to both (mortal in Pacer's case) they manage to meet for a final reunion.

Reviews This is almost unique in being liked by the critics but low on the fans' list of favorites, possibly due to the lack of songs. Reviewers were moved to say such things as "gives Presley a good role and he makes the most of it . . . script makes some cogent points concerning peace among men."

74

WILD IN THE COUNTRY *(1961)*

20th Century Fox

Glenn	*Elvis*
Irene	*Hope Lange*
Noreen	*Tuesday Weld*
Betty Lee	*Millie Perkins*
Phil Macy	*John Ireland*
Producer	*Jerry Wald*
Director	*Philip Dunne*

Songs

I Slipped, I Stumbled, I Fell; In My Way; Wild In The Country

Synopsis

The story hangs around the troubles experienced by Glenn, an aspiring young writer who gets an undeserved reputation for violence. He is ordered to visit a psychiatrist, Irene Sperry, regularly and she, together with his girlfriend Betty Lee, encourages him in his literary ambitions. Unfortunately, he has made enemies, not least of them his Uncle Rolfe and a worthless scoundrel, Cliff, son of a wealthy lawyer Phil Macy who wants to marry Irene. The already simmering passions are raised to boiling point by some complicated romantic entanglements and Cliff, wanting to spite Glenn, adds to resentments by spreading rumors about his relationship with Irene. Glenn hot-headedly swears revenge and on meeting his antagonist a fight ensues as a result of which Cliff, who has a weak heart, dies. Glenn is arrested and, when it seems he will be found guilty because Macy withholds vital medical evidence about his son's condition, Irene attempts suicide. This brings everyone to their senses. Glenn is acquitted and goes to college to pursue his writing career.

Reviews

The critics seem unanimous in their apathy with such expressions as "boring" and "oh dear" figuring in the notices. Renowned US critic Judith Crist commented: "Elvis Presley gets stuck in a bowl of goo . . . He outacts everyone around — but that's faint praise."

BLUE HAWAII *(1961)*

Paramount

Chad Gates	*Elvis*
Maile Duval	*Joan Blackman*
Sarah Lee Gates	*Angela Lansbury*
Abigail Prentace	*Nancy Walters*
Producer	*Hal Wallis*
Director	*Norman Taurog*

Songs   Blue Hawaii; Almost Always True; Aloha-Oe; No More; Can't Help Falling In Love; Rock-A-Hula Baby; Moonlight Swim; Ku-U-I-Po (Hawaiian Sweetheart); Ito Eats; Slicin' Sand; Hawaiian Sunset; Beach Boy Blues; Island Of Love; Hawaiian Wedding Song

Synopsis   Chad Gates is a happy-go-lucky beach boy whose job as tourist guide to a school-marm and her four female charges involves him in a complex romantic entanglement and successive series of misunderstandings which keep him hopping between his girlfriend Maile (of whom his mother

disapproves), a spoilt precocious school-girl, Ellie and Abigail the chaperone. His endeavors to keep all these women professionally and romantically happy land him in a succession of quandaries before the misapprehensions are explained and true love takes its satisfactory course.

Reviews

The critics seemed to be agreed that this was a pleasant film which they mostly dismissed with expressions like "mild," "has little else except Presley and pretty pictures," and "for those with a special appreciation of palm trees, pineapples and Presley." However, the fans loved it and it is frequently quoted as being his most successful movie. *Variety,* however, disputes this in its 1976 "All-Time Film Rental Champs" listings and places it second most popular after *Viva Las Vegas* and 503rd in overall ranking with US/Canada rental receipts of $4,700,000; this figure does *not* reflect tickets bought at the box-office and it is possible that this is Elvis's most-viewed film.

FOLLOW THAT DREAM (1962)

United Artists

Toby Kwimper	*Elvis*
Pop Kwimper	*Arthur O'Connell*
Holly Jones	*Anne Helm*
Alicia Claypoole	*Joanna Moore*
Producer	*David Weisbart*
Director	*Gordon Douglas*

Songs

What A Wonderful Life; I'm Not The Marrying Kind; Sound Advice; Follow That Dream; Angel; On Top Of Old Smokey

Synopsis

Pop Kwimper and his son Toby are family to four orphans ranging from Holly, 19, down to Ariadne, three. Searching for somewhere to settle they stop by a highway and, when officious bureaucracy tries to move them on, decide to homestead. Despite the authorities' attempts to evict them, the family establish a little community of trailers. Attracted to the area — which falls outside police jurisdiction — is a gambler who sets up a mobile casino and turns the site into a den of iniquity. The other 'citizens' elect Toby sheriff and he gives the gambler notice to quit. The gangster brings in hoods to rub out Toby but through luck and courage he gets the better of them and, having cleaned up the new township, assists the rest of the family in their successful fight to remain together.

Reviews

Opinion was divided as to the movie's merits and, particularly, Elvis's acting. On one hand there was the "strictly for Presley fans" comment that was to become so familiar, on the other hand it was "a genuinely entertaining comedy. It remains Presley's pleasantest performance." And while one critic waspishly asserted that "Elvis sings without wiggling in this one, although sometimes he scratches" a true devotee loyally proclaimed "this is the kind of movie which deserves an Oscar."

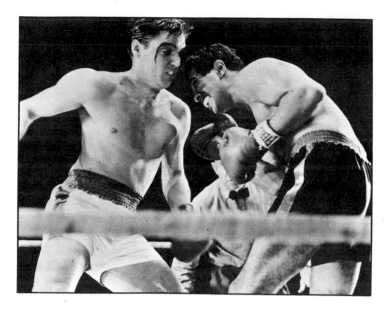

KID GALAHAD (1962)

United Artists

Walter Gulick	*Elvis*
Willy Grogan	*Gig Young*
Dolly Fletcher	*Lola Albright*
Rose Grogan	*Joan Blackman*
Lew Nyack	*Charles Bronson*
Producer	*David Weisbart*
Director	*Phil Karlson*

Songs

King Of The Whole Wide World; This Is Living; Riding The Rainbow; Home Is Where The Heart Is; I Got Lucky; A Whistling Tune

Synopsis

A strong supporting cast backed up Elvis who played a recently demobbed GI who fetches up at a boxers' training camp and, having taken a job as sparring partner, shows an amazing talent as a fighter. Promoted by Willy Grogan who urgently needs money, and in love with Willy's sister Rose, Walter becomes Kid Galahad, quick KO specialist and local hero. He's only in the game for the money and, as soon as he can, he intends to get out, buy a business and settle down with Rose. His last fight is to be against a tough and experienced fighter who's run by Otto Danzig, a ruthless gambler determined to make a killing even if he has to threaten, menace or bribe Kid's people to throw the fight. Danzig's pressures are resisted, Kid floors his man and all, inevitably, ends happily.

Reviews

Despite the presence of Gig Young (who won an Oscar for *They Shoot Horses Don't They?*) and the soon-to-be-immensely-popular Bronson, this found little favor with the critics, probably because many remembered the earlier version starring Edward G Robinson and Bette Davis which was considered to be one of the finest fight movies ever made. "A dismal remake of the 1937 classic," commented one. "Young and Lola Albright . . . struggle valiantly but vainly in this mess." A reviewer representing Elvis's fan club disagreed: "A perfect foil for the Presley magic and shows how experienced an actor Elvis has become."

GIRLS! GIRLS! GIRLS! (1962)

Paramount

Ross Carpenter	*Elvis*
Robin Gantner	*Stella Stevens*
Laurel Dodge	*Laurel Goodwin*
Wesley Johnson	*Jeremy Slate*
Producer	*Hal Wallis*
Director	*Norman Taurog*

Songs

Girls! Girls! Girls!; I Don't Wanna Be Tied; I Don't Want To; We'll Be Together; A Boy Like Me, A Girl Like You; Earth Boy; Return To Sender; Because Of Love; Thanks To The Rolling Sea; Song Of The Shrimp; The Walls Have Ears; We're Coming In Loaded. Stella Stevens sang Baby, Baby, Baby; Never Let Me Go and The Nearness Of You

Synopsis

The similarities between this and *Blue Hawaii* are strong and feature much the same sort of misunderstandings. Ross Carpenter's great love is the *West Wind*, the fishing boat he skippers and one day hopes to own. Unfortunately the boat's owner who is sympathetic to Ross's ambition is forced to sell *West Wind* to Wesley Johnson a hard-nosed businessman who doubles the boat's price. Robin Gantner, a nightclub singer, is in love with Ross but he has fallen for Laurel Dodge, the daughter of a wealthy man who, unbeknownst to Ross, buys the boat as a gift to him. When he learns this Ross is furious, refuses to accept "charity" and storms off. Laurel sets after him in the boat which is crewed by Johnson, Ross mistakes his boss's intentions, boards the vessel and attacks him. Swiftly, however, the confusions are solved, Ross and Laurel reunited and peace reigns.

Reviews

Critical opinion proved almost unanimous on this one with most commentators adopting the "Elvis sings and swings his way through this harmless piece of fluff" line. The old "strictly for Presley fans" cliché appeared along with such opinion as: "Featherweight item about fishing boats." However, at least one film historian has considered that, in retrospect, it is "one of his better pictures" and committed Elvis opinion claims "*nothing* can prevent it from being one of the Elvis Film Classics."

IT HAPPENED AT THE WORLD'S FAIR
(1963)
M.G.M.

Mike Edwards	*Elvis*
Diane Warren	*Joan O'Brien*
Danny Burke	*Gary Lockwood*
Producer	*Ted Richmond*
Director	*Norman Taurog*

Songs

Beyond The Bend; Relax; Take Me To The Fair; They Remind Me Too Much Of You; One Broken Heart For Sale; I'm Falling In Love Tonight; Cotton Candy; A World Of Our Own; How Would You Like To Be; Happy Ending

Synopsis

Mike and Danny are two pilots who between their respective obsessions for girls and gambling find themselves penniless and planeless. A search for work takes them to Seattle and the World's Fair where Mike meets Sue-Lin, a little Chinese girl, and her Uncle Walter and Danny searches for a shady friend, Vince, who might offer a charter. When Uncle Walter is forced to abandon the visit to the Fair in favor of business Mike steps in as Sue-Lin's escort and meets Diane, a pretty nurse for whom he makes an unsuccessful play. Trouble ensues when Uncle Walter goes missing and Sue Lin is claimed by the welfare board but escapes from custody. Meanwhile Danny has found a commission but he and Mike become suspicious about Vince's cargo and, discovering it to be contraband furs, a fight ensues which ends in the crooks' arrest. Uncle Walter is found safe and Mike gets Diane with whom he enlists for the aerospace program!

Reviews

It is true to say that commentators loathed this movie and perhaps British critic Elkan Allan summed up their feelings when he said: "If it didn't have Elvis Presley in it, this could be dismissed as a lousy film that desperately uses the World's Fairground in an effort to inject some novelty. With Elvis, it's a lousy film with ten musical numbers that desperately uses the World's Fairground . . ." A reviewer for Elvis's Fan Club took, understandably, a different line: "Elvis ACTS (yes, film critics, *acts*) all the way through this gem of celluloid masterpiece" but admitted that it was "not the right script" for the star.

FUN IN ACAPULCO (1963)
Paramount

Mike Windgren	*Elvis*
Margarita Dauphine	*Ursula Andress*
Dolores Gomez	*Elsa Cardenas*
Maximillian	*Paul Lukas*
Producer	*Hal Wallis*
Director	*Richard Thorpe*

Songs

Fun In Acapulco; Vino, Dinero y Amor; Mexico; El Toro; Margarita; The Bullfighter Was A Lady; There's No Room To Rhumba In A Sports Car; I Think I'm Gonna Like It Here; Bossa Nova Baby; You Can't Say No In Acapulco; Guadalajara

Synopsis

Mike, escaping from a trapeze accident that injured his partner, arrives in Acapulco where he gets a job as a singer by night, pool lifeguard by day and falls for Margarita. Moreno, another lifeguard who also dives 130ft from cliff to sea each night, loves Margarita too and determines to win her by capitalizing on Mike's fear of heights. Mike and Moreno fight, the latter pretends to be too hurt to dive and Mike, fighting to overcome the guilt and fear that grip him, takes his place. Courage triumphs, the dive is successful, Mike wins the girl.

Reviews

Despite the inclusion of a big-name glamor girl (Miss Andress was fresh from her success in *Dr No*) instead of the usual unknown lovely, the critics did not warm to this outing. "What distinguishes this from myriad other Presley films," asserted one, "is the nifty scenery." He was referring to Ursula. Another was blind even to these charms: "Presley might have had some fun counting the money . . . from this rotten movie, but it doesn't extend to us." A spokesman for the fans, however, generally liked it: "While Elvis makes these sort of films, his popularity will be as strong — family-wise — as ever."

VIVA LAS VEGAS! (1964)

M.G.M.
(retitled UK: Love In Las Vegas)

Lucky Jackson	*Elvis*
Rusty Martin	*Ann-Margret*
Count Mancini	*Cesare Donova*
Mr. Martin	*William Demarest*
Producer	*Jack Cummings/George Sidney*
Director	*George Sidney*

Songs

I Need Somebody To Lean On; The Yellow Rose Of Texas; Viva Las Vegas; The Lady Loves Me; What'd I Say; C'mon Everybody; If You Think I Don't Need You; Today, Tomorrow And Forever; Santa Lucia; The Eyes Of Texas. The Rival and Appreciation both sung by Ann-Margret

Synopsis

Lucky is an ambitious racing driver who arrives in Vegas for a Grand Prix, establishes a professional rivalry with Mancini and falls for Rusty. He loses the money intended for a new engine and takes a waiter's job which entitles him to enter a talent contest. He wins but receives a gold cup and Monaco trip instead of cash. His racing chances are in jeopardy but Rusty's rich father comes to the financial rescue in the nick of time and, after a furious drive, Lucky wins both the race and Rusty.

Reviews

Surprisingly, this is Elvis's most successful film according to *Variety*'s 1976 table of "All-Time Film Rental Champs" which is a list of all movies that have received over $4,000,000 in rentals to the distributor in US and Canada only and should not be confused with box-office grosses. It ranked 429 (out of nearly 700 entries) with receipts totalling $5,152,000. This popularity was reflected in a rather warmer critical reception of which "it's fast, painless and one of Elvis's brighter vehicles" is typical. It is agreed that the movie benefitted from Ann-Margret's vivacious and energetic presence.

KISSIN' COUSINS (1964)

M.G.M.

Josh Morgan	*Elvis*
Jodie Tatum	
Pappy Tatum	*Arthur O'Connell*
Ma Tatum	*Glenda Farrell*
Capt. Robert Salbo	*Jack Albertson*
Producer	*Sam Katzman*
Director	*Gene Nelson*

Songs

Smokey Mountain Boy; Once Is Enough; Kissin' Cousins; One Boy, Two Little Girls; Tender Feelin'; Catchin' On Fast; There's Gold In The Mountains; Barefoot Ballad; Pappy, Won't You Please Come Home (sung by Glenda Farrell)

Synopsis

The Air Force wants to build a missile base on the mountain that Pappy Tatum owns and which houses his illicit 'moonshine' still. Thinking its representatives are revenue men he and son Jodie repulse them with shotguns and, in desperation, the Service resorts to enlisting the help of local boy, Lt. Josh Morgan. He gets to the Tatums and all are astonished to find that Josh and Jodie are doubles — the result of unsuspected kinship. While Josh, Jodie and others are becoming romantically involved, Pappy finally agrees to leasing the mountain to the USAF in return for protection of his still from revenue men.

Reviews

"Elvis in a dual role, which is either too much or not enough, depending on one's outlook." Many critics adopted this approach and considered that the movie and its plot were routine. A fan club critic was far more enthusiastic: "The situations these Kissin' Cousins got into were a real riot . . . and the novelty of having two Elvis's . . . was a real sight to behold."

ROUSTABOUT *(1964)*

Paramount

Charlie Rogers	*Elvis*
Maggie Moore	*Barbara Stanwyck*
Cathy Lean	*Joan Freeman*
Joe Lean	*Leif Erickson*
Producer	*Hal Wallis*
Director	*John Rich*

Songs

Roustabout; Poison Ivy League; Wheels On My Heels; It's Carnival Time; Carnie Town; One Track Heart; Hard Knocks; Little Egypt; Big Love, Big Heartache; There's A Brand New Day On The Horizon; It's A Wonderful World

Synopsis

Charlie, a free-wheeling, singing karate expert, hooks up with a rundown carnival, is attracted to Cathy, antagonizes her father Joe and revitalizes business with his singing. Just as things are looking rosy a series of misfortunes and misunderstandings make it seem that Charlie is an ungrateful heel and he leaves to accept an offer from a rival outfit. Cathy still loves him, however, and persuades him back to save the carnival from bankruptcy. Charlie and Joe settle their differences in a spirited fight, the golden voice pulls in the crowds and all augurs well for romance.

Reviews

Although some critics despaired that Barbara Stanwyck, star of such fine films as *Double Indemnity, Meet John Doe* and *Ball Of Fire* should "descend" to this, and most dismissed it as "another Presley opus for his fans" there were those who subscribed to one view that it was "slightly improved jollity." And while his most ardent fans obviously agreed with a club spokesman that it was "full of life and boisterous" with "strong acting by Elvis" they may have been taken aback by his contention that "this is the worst crop of songs . . . that Elvis has had to contend with."

GIRL HAPPY *(1965)*

M.G.M.

Rusty Wells	*Elvis*
Valerie	*Shelley Fabares*
Big Frank	*Harold J Stone*
Andy	*Gary Crosby*
Producer	*Joe Pasternak*
Director	*Boris Segal*

Songs

Girl Happy; Spring Fever; Fort Lauderdale Chamber Of Commerce; Startin' Tonight; Wolf Call; Do Not Disturb; Cross My Heart And Hope To Die; The Meanest Girl In Town; Puppet On A String; I've Got To Find My Baby. Read All About It sung by Shelley Fabares/Nita Talbot

Synopsis

Rusty and his group are ordered by Chicago club boss Big Frank to act as unobtrusive chaperones to his daughter, Valerie, when they all go to Florida. Rusty finds it increasingly difficult to watch Valerie and date other girls but the problem resolves itself when they fall in love. Unfortunately, Valerie learns of Rusty's watchdog role, objects, gets drunk, does a strip and is arrested. Rusty tunnels into jail to rescue her but discovers Big Frank has already bailed her out, is himself held and escapes by donning a woman's disguise. The ending is, unsurprisingly, happy.

Reviews

The fact that the plots of Presley movies were showing increasing signs of thinness was not missed even by the most uncomplaining admirer. Even a fan club reviewer felt compelled to say of this: "One of a dozen Elvis movies which has a story line not different enough to stand out in your mind." The same writer thought the songs and most scenes unmemorable. Other critics agreed and comments like "the whole shebang is strictly a matter of taste" were common.

TICKLE ME (1965)

Allied Artists

Lonnie Beale	*Elvis*
Vera Radford	*Julie Adams*
Pam Merritt	*Jocelyn Lane*
Stanley Potter	*Jack Mullaney*
Producer	*Ben Schwalb*
Director	*Norman Taurog*

Songs

I Feel That I've Known You Forever; Night Rider; Slowly, But Surely; Dirty, Dirty Feeling; Put The Blame On Me; Long, Lonely Highway; I'm Yours; Such An Easy Question; It Feels So Right.

Synopsis

Singing cowboy Lonnie lands a job at a health ranch for women where his success is largely due to his sexual magnetism. Ironically, the only girl who is cool to his charm is Pam, the one he loves and the heir to a fortune in gold hidden in a nearby ghost town. Pam warms to Lonnie when he saves her from a masked intruder who attempts to rob her of the cryptic clues to the treasure's hiding place. Their love is jeopardized when Pam finds Lonnie in a compromising position and won't accept his pleas of innocence. Dejected Lonnie goes back, unsuccessfully, to the rodeo circuit until summoned by friend Stanley to aid Pam in the gold search. Marooned in the ghost town Lonnie foils two crooks' efforts to get the gold, saves Pam and Stanley accidentally discovers the treasure.

Reviews

"Deadly" was the adjective applied by one critic to this movie and a further reviewer observed that "his fans won't mind, but Elvis deserves better than this skimpy little nothing." His fans, judging by the opinion of one of their spokesmen, didn't mind: "full marks for an exciting, laugh-packed thriller, with situations getting zanier all the time."

HARUM SCARUM (1965)

M.G.M.

(retitled UK: Harem Holiday)

Johnny Tyrone	*Elvis*
Princess Shalimar	*Mary Ann Mobley*
Aishah	*Fran Jeffries*
Prince Dragma	*Michael Ansara*
Producer	*Sam Katzman*
Director	*Gene Nelson*

Songs

Harem Holiday; My Desert Serenade; Go East — Young Man; Mirage; Kismet; Shake That Tambourine; Hey Little Girl; Golden Coins; So Close, Yet So Far. Animal Instinct and Wisdom Of The Ages were cut from most prints.

Synopsis

Johnny Tyrone is a movie singing star who is kidnapped by a band of assassins whilst on tour in the Middle East. He escapes with the aid of a troupe of entertainers and meets a beautiful princess (who he believes is a mere slavegirl), the daughter of the Sheikh the assassins intend to kill. Johnny is eventually recaptured by the killers who hold his friends hostage against his failure to kill the Sheikh himself. Caught in this quandary of conflicting loyalties Johnny is powerless to resist the kidnappers' demands until the troupe and the Princess come to his aid and together they are able to rout the evil-doers, save the Sheikh's life and still get to a nearby nightclub to fulfill a cabaret engagement!

Reviews

No one would claim that this is one of Elvis's better efforts and some would and did condemn it as "plodding" and "even for Elvis's fans this is a little much." The formidable Judith Crist was rather kinder: "Miss Mobley is pretty (but Yvonne DeCarlo she's not), Elvis wears a burnoose (but Valentino he's not) . . . decent, wholesome stuff." Perhaps a fan club reviewer summed it up best with: "No better and no worse than some of Elvis's previous films but the fact that there were so many just the same seemed to make fans a little apathetic towards this particular movie."

FRANKIE AND JOHNNY (1966)

United Artists

Johnny	*Elvis*
Frankie	*Donna Douglas*
Nellie Bly	*Nancy Kovack*
Clint Braden	*Anthony Eisley*
Producer	*Edward Small*
Director	*Frederick De Cordova*

Songs

Everybody Come Aboard; Frankie And Johnny; Come Along; Petunia, The Gardener's Daughter; Chesay; What Every Woman Lives For; Look Out Broadway; Beginner's Luck; Down By The Riverside/ When The Saints; Shout It Out; Hard Luck; Please Don't Stop Loving Me

Synopsis

Based loosely on the traditional song, this tells of a singing team, Frankie and Johnny, who work on a Mississippi showboat. Frankie loves Johnny but Johnny loves gambling and, being very superstitious, he is attracted to Nellie Bly, a red-head whom he believes will bring true a prophesy. This makes Frankie and their boss, Clint — who loves Nellie — jealous and by tragic mischance a live bullet is loaded into the gun that Frankie uses at the climax of their act featuring the title song to 'shoot' Johnny. Fortunately, the bullet strikes Johnny's lucky mascot and he is unharmed. In the general relief all the other misunderstandings are sorted out to everyone's satisfaction.

Reviews

The acerbic American critic Judith Crist was particularly caustic about this: "Not up to even his formularized standards, with little exploitation of the possibilities of plot, production numbers or period . . . low-ebb effort that seems scriptless, directionless and virtually tuneless." Others thought it "shoddy" but one opined backhandedly that "as Presley vehicles go this one isn't too awful" and another considered it "returned somewhat to primitive quality of his early films." The faithful, however, thought it "just the right vehicle for Elvis."

PARADISE, HAWAIIAN STYLE (1966)

Paramount

Rick Richards	*Elvis*
Judy Hudson	*Suzanna Leigh*
Danny Kohana	*James Shigeta*
Producer	*Hal Wallis*
Director	*Michael Moore*

Songs

Paradise, Hawaiian Style; House Of Sand; Queenie Wahine's Papaya; You Scratch My Back; Drums Of The Island; It's A Dog's Life; Dating; Stop, Where You Are; This Is My Heaven. Bill Bailey, Won't You Please Come Home sung by Donna Butterworth

Synopsis

Rick is an unemployed pilot who returns home to Hawaii to enlist the aid of friend Danny in a helicopter charter company. Danny is unenthusiastic because he knows Rick is easily diverted from business by pretty girls but eventually falls in with his friend's plan for persuading all his girl-friends to recruit clients. Judy Hudson joins the team and is cool towards Rick especially when he nearly crashes his chopper into the car of a Federal Aviation Agent and endangers his licence. Her opinion of him is not improved when he sets off for a joyride with Danny's daughter that goes wrong, marooning them overnight and worries Danny so much that he dissolves the partnership. Later Danny and daughter go missing and Rick risks losing his licence by searching for and rescuing them. His loyalty is noted by the authorities, the licence restored and Judy defrosted.

Reviews

The similarity to *Blue Hawaii* in locations and other movies in plots were not missed by critics who came out with such phrases as "tired old repetition of all his previous films." The indomitable Miss Crist was damning: "If you want goo on top of bland white bread, it's there for the spreading." Even fans had their grumbles and perhaps the best that could be said was: "Definitely a film to sit back and enjoy Elvis enjoying. He couldn't keep a smile off his face!"

SPINOUT *(1966)*

M.G.M.
(retitled UK: California Holiday)

Mike McCoy	*Elvis*
Cynthia Foxhugh	*Shelley Fabares*
Diana St. Clare	*Diane McBain*
Producer	*Joe Pasternak*
Director	*Norman Taurog*

Songs

Stop, Look And Listen; Adam and Evil; All That I Am; Never Say Yes; Am I Ready; Beach Shack; Smorgasbord; I'll Be Back; Spinout

Synopsis

Mike is a carefree singing racing driver who is being chased by three girls — rich man's daughter Cynthia, author Diana who's researching *The Perfect American Male* and duckling-turned-swan female drummer Les — and by Cynthia's father, Howard Foxhugh, who wants him to drive a new car in an upcoming race. By some quick thinking Mike manages to avoid all the pressures, both marital and business, win the race (but not for Foxhugh) and play matchmaker for the three pursuing girls.

Reviews

By now many people thought that the rot was really setting in and that Presley movies were being ground out on some studio treadmill. The critics seemed too disinterested even to make wisecracks and settled for languid ''below par Pelvis'' or ''weak . . . does him no good, nor us neither.'' The indefatigable Presley supporter could find some merit though: ''An enjoyable family film with Elvis vocally and visually on top form.''

EASY COME, EASY GO (1967)

Paramount

Ted Jackson	*Elvis*
Whitehead	*Mickey Elley*
Tompkins	*Reed Morgan*
Producer	*Hal Wallis*
Director	*John Rich*

Songs

Easy Come, Easy Go; The Love Machine; You Gotta Stop; Sing You Children; Yoga Is As Yoga Does; I'll Take Love

Synopsis

Lt. Ted Jackson is a Navy diver who discovers an old wreck while on routine duties. Hoping to learn more about the sunken ship he consults a local expert, Jo Symington, who is a beautiful hippie and disapproves of his mercenary intentions. Unfortunately, someone else has learned of the wreck, the race is on and his rival will stop at nothing to win. After overcoming many difficulties and an underwater fight, Ted raises the treasure chest to discover it is full of copper coins and worth very little, but what does money matter when you've got love in the shape of an uninhibited hippie?

Reviews

It was considered to be stereotyped but inoffensive and elicited better notices for Elvis than the plot which was thought "aimless." His acting was considered by one critic to be "better than the dopey script" and Judith Crist, ever endeavoring to be fair, thought Elvis managed "to rise a teensy bit above his mediocre material." Official fan opinion was little better, the songs were "not masterpieces," and the editing "seemed to hide Elvis" and the conclusion was that "if remembered for anything it will be for the zany situations and glossy photography."

DOUBLE TROUBLE (1967)

M.G.M.

Guy Lambert	*Elvis*
Jill Conway	*Annette Day*
Gerald Waverly	*John Williams*
Claire Dunham	*Yvonne Romain*
Producer	*Judd Bernard/Irwin Winkler*
Director	*Norman Taurog*

Songs

Double Trouble; Baby If You'll Give Me All Your Love; City By Night; There's So Much World To See; Could I Fall In Love; Long Legged Girl; Old MacDonald; I Love Only One Girl

Synopsis

Unwittingly Guy Lambert gets involved in an extremely complex plot that involves the beautiful Jill, her guardian Gerald, a rich playgirl, some suspicious followers and all sorts of crosses, double-crosses, murder attempts and a great many people who aren't what they seem. The action takes place in England and Belgium and even a publication dedicated entirely to Elvis and his works is baffled by the twists in the plot and especially the denouement of which its harassed reviewer writes: "utter confusion reigns at this point, when everything should have been settled and explained."

Reviews

Inexplicably, and for the first time, the reviewers and the official spokesman swap roles. The critics generally thought it "better than average" while the poor bemused fan club viewer complained that "the whole production was very slapdash and not least of this was the songs" and asserted that "surely no one would claim that there was one notable scene in this muddle."

CLAMBAKE (1967)

United Artists

Scott Heyward	*Elvis*
Dianne Carter	*Shelley Fabares*
Tom Wilson	*Will Hutchins*
James Jamison	*Bill Bixby*
Duster Heywood	*James Gregory*
Sam Burton	*Gary Merrill*
Producer	*Levy-Gardner-Laven Productions*
Director	*Arthur Nadel*

Songs

Clambake; Who Needs Money?; A House That Has Everything; Confidence; Hey, Hey, Hey; You Don't Know Me; The Girl I Never Loved

Synopsis

Scott Heyward is heir to millions but is tired of getting everything except what he really wants — independence and the chance to prove his own abilities as a research scientist. He runs away from his father and unearned promotion and swaps identities with a water ski instructor at a Miami Beach hotel. He meets gold-digging Dianne who's out to land a rich husband and offers to help in her campaign to net millionaire powerboat racer Jamison but becomes jealous when the plan starts to work. To catch Dianne's attention he persuades one of Jamison's rival boat owners to let him fix a deadly design flaw in the racer's hull with an untested, volatile coating he developed for his father's company and drive the boat in the race. In the meantime, Scott's father has discovered his whereabouts and Dianne has seen the error of her ways; now perfection depends on Scott winning despite the unproven qualities of his bonding agent. Will the boat's hull smash apart under pressure, killing Scott? It won't!

Reviews

The film was met with overwhelming critical apathy and comments like "dull" and even "oh dear!" Even the most hardened of Presley movie-goers was only able to advise his devoted readers to "stand and watch this one go by."

SPEEDWAY (1968)

M.G.M.

Steve Gregson	*Elvis*
Susan Jacks	*Nancy Sinatra*
Producer	*Douglas Laurence*
Director	*Norman Taurog*

Songs

Speedway; There Ain't Nothing Like A Song; Your Time Hasn't Come Yet Baby; Who Are You?; He's Your Uncle Not Your Dad; Let Yourself Go. Your Groovy Self sung by Nancy Sinatra

Synopsis

Steve Gregson's success at motor racing allows him to indulge his love of handing out money to deserving causes. Unfortunately this generosity lands him in problems because he hasn't been paying his taxes and owes the Revenue a fortune. He takes on an accountant to handle his finances and although she's young and extremely lovely the conflict in their personalities spells romantic doom. A series of set-backs force Steve to consider selling his beloved racing car to raise enough cash to pay off his personal obligations if not his tax but in the nick of time Susan negotiates a time extension with the taxman and so he's able to enter the Daytona 500 even though he crashes just before crossing the finishing line.

Reviews

This movie was so little thought of that in Britain — traditionally Presley's strongest and most devoted market — it was put into theaters as a second feature, the first time an Elvis movie had suffered such humiliation. Adjectives like "tiresome" and "bore" dragged their way from the tired typewriters of weary critics and even the most flattering pro-Presley commentator was crushed: "The plot took 40 minutes to develop and as it arrived was treated so lightly that when there was no conclusion it was not unexpected . . . No wonder it was the first second feature Elvis film in England."

STAY AWAY JOE (1968)
M.G.M.

Joe Lightcloud	*Elvis*
Glenda Callahan	*Joan Blondell*
Charlie Lightcloud	*Burgess Meredith*
Annie Lightcloud	*Katy Jurado*
Producer	*Douglas Laurence*
Director	*Peter Tewksbury*

Songs

All I Needed Was The Rain; Stay Away Joe; Dominique

Synopsis

Joe Lightcloud, who lives on an Indian reservation and prefers to spend his time riding bulls and motor bikes, is given $20 plus a young bull by the government to enable him to start a herd. After a catastrophic series of events, including the collapse of his mother's recently acquired indoor plumbing, he throws a wild party at which the bull gets mistaken for a cow and killed for food. Joe finally saves enough for a new one by selling his car, piece by piece, and winning a bull-riding competition. The movie ends with a massive fight in which Joe's house collapses, only for him to emerge from the rubble to say: "Sure was one hell of a fight."

Reviews

If reviewers had been apathetic about some of Elvis's previous efforts they were downright vitriolic about this. "Stay away, whatever your name is!;" "Tacky slapstick;" "Custer himself might be embarrassed — for the Indians;" "Even fanatics will find it one of Presley's shabbiest films;" "A sad, boring effort." The fanatics weren't enamored of the movie: "Good to look at, if a little noisy, but was there a point to it all?" This antipathy was reflected by the trade in Britain where it wasn't even given a national release.

LIVE A LITTLE, LOVE A LITTLE (1968)
M.G.M.

Greg Nolan	*Elvis*
Bernice	*Michele Carey*
Harry	*Dick Sargent*
Mike Lansdown	*Don Porter*
Penlow	*Rudy Vallee*
Producer	*Douglas Laurence*
Director	*Norman Taurog*

Songs

Wonderful World; Edge Of Reality; A Little Less Conversation; Almost In Love

Synopsis

Greg, a photographer on an LA paper, has his privacy and independence invaded by Bernice and a Great Dane called Albert. He catches pneumonia but with Bernice looking after him, sleeps for three days and loses his job. She also moves him out of his apartment and in with her. Greg gets a job as a commercial photographer for two opposing firms located in the same building. Because one boss is formal and the other is casual he has to constantly adjust his appearance. Bernice finds him a new house and has to move in but there is only one bedroom and after a

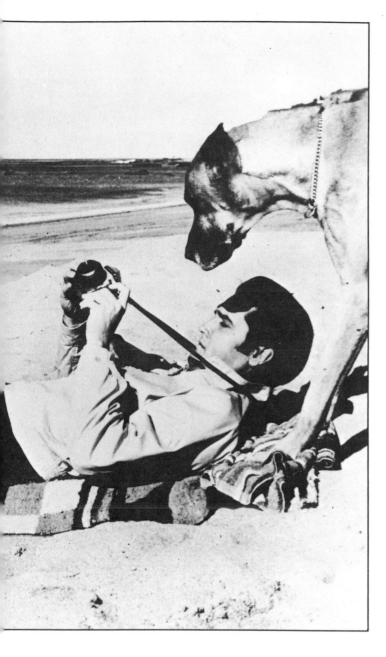

THE TROUBLE WITH GIRLS (1969)
M.G.M.

Walter Hale	*Elvis*
Nita	*Sheree North*
Johnny Anthony	*Edward Andrews*
Charlene	*Marlyn Mason*
Producer	*Lester Welch*
Director	*Peter Tewksbury*

Songs   Almost; Swing Low Sweet Chariot; Clean Up Your Own Back Yard

Synopsis   Walter Hale is the youthful manager of a chatauqua — a travelling academy or 'Rolling Canvas College' — in the '20s. The show hits Radford Center and affects the lives of the people there. Some see it as a way out of small town life but for others it brings tragedy especially when Wilby, the town pharmacist is murdered and a gambler is arrested. Walter Hale — in between being vamped by town girls hoping to join his show and love-hating the staunchly feminist Charlene — solves the mystery and turns the unmasking of the murderer into his greatest performance ever.

"period of restraint" the inevitable happens. Bernice, confused, runs away but Greg chases after her to declare undying love, as a result of which they all live happily ever after.

Reviews   Things were going from bad to worse and, increasingly, Presley looked as if he was simply going through paces. The scripts and production values as well as the number and standard of songs were all steadily falling, and it's a mystery why Rudy Vallee — crooning idol of the '20s and star of such comedy classics as *The Palm Beach Story* and *The Bachelor And The Bobbysoxer* — ever got involved with this. Presley, presumably, was on contract. Judith Crist sums it up with typical zest: "Only the most devout Presleyites will be enchanted . . . it shortchanges him and them, what with only a couple of songs and a completely incoherent plot." Unsurprisingly, it was never distributed in Britain where even those most devout Presleyites were not turning up in enough numbers at cinemas to make it worth booking.

Reviews   The humiliations suffered by Elvis's two previous films in Britain were continued when 25 minutes were cut out of this one. But, on the whole, the critics didn't look too unkindly on this rather untypical movie. One considered it "a notch or two above most of his films of the '60s;" another thought it "one of Presley's pleasantest vehicles and a good deal of unpretentious fun." A fan club reviewer, doubtless stung by the lack of success that Presley films were achieving, tried to spotlight the reason: "Elvis at his most handsome maybe but the general public require more than that to encourage them to pay for another look."

brother of Vince, the gang leader, who gets drunk, wounds the sheriff and is jailed by Jess. Vince demands his brother's release and threatens to open fire on the town with the cannon if he's not free by sundown. The deadlock is broken by the commencement of shelling and Jess's determination to get even; he rides out to face Vince's men and wins the upper hand in a fierce showdown. The cannon is recaptured and returned and Jess rides off into the setting sun.

Reviews

This was probably Presley's first serious stab at playing a straight role since *Flaming Star* and although there was a change of image in that he wore, and looked well in, a beard the critics were not very impressed. One brusquely advised him to "stop trying to act, and sing." His loyal, but dwindling, band of filmgoers were informed by their correspondent that "Elvis's ability stood out for the cast as a whole were poor. This poorness applied to the technical aspects also . . . and was ample reason for the critics to slate it and Elvis."

CHANGE OF HABIT *(1969)*
Universal

Dr. John Carpenter	*Elvis*
Sister Michelle	*Mary Tyler Moore*
Sister Irene	*Barbara McNair*
Sister Barbara	*Jane Elliot*
Producer	*Joe Connelly*
Director	*William Graham*

Songs

Change Of Habit; Rubberneckin'; Let Us Pray; Have A Happy

Synopsis

Three nuns, out of habit and incognito, arrive in a tough ghetto to assist the local social workers one of whom is Dr. John Carpenter. Their foray into the community is an experiment that, at first, seems to work despite the antipathy of the diehard local priest. However, things soon go awry when Carpenter starts falling in love with Sister Michelle and cannot understand why she keeps rebuffing him, black Sister Irene finds the plight of her people demands a radical commitment and Sister Barbara finds her political beliefs in conflict with those of her calling. The nuns are ordered to either return to their convent or resume the wearing of habit. Michelle and Irene adopt the latter course and Carpenter finds himself in the dilemma of loving a nun. Each have to reassess their attitudes and nothing is resolved.

Reviews

Despite a very much more modern storyline and the advantage of having in Mary Tyler Moore Elvis's best-known co-star for many years, this film fared no better than his immediately preceding features. In fact, in Britain it got no theater release at all and had the very dubious honor of being the first US film to have its British premiere on television. The ratings did not show any particular excitement among viewers at the event. Such reviews as it

CHARRO *(1969)*
National General

Jess Wade	*Elvis*
Tracy	*Ina Balin*
Vince	*Victor French*
Producer/Director	*Charles M Warren*

Songs

Charro

Synopsis

Jess Wade is lured into a trap set by his former outlaw friends who show him the Mexican Victory Cannon — embellished with silver and gold — that they have stolen and warn him that they are circulating false wanted posters connecting him with the crime on both sides of the border. To complete the identification — the poster describes the scar of a severe neck wound that was received in the course of the raid — they brand Jess with a poker. Outcast and hunted by two countries' lawmen Jess seeks refuge in a town where the sheriff is a friend and does not believe he is guilty. Into the town comes the crazed

received were non-committal and tended to describe it as "mild." Fan reviews made the best of it all with comments like: "Acting standards are higher and the song content lower. All the elements of a good role are present — comedy, drama, suspense and most of all Doctor Elvis makes a welcome change from Playboy Elvis."

ELVIS — THAT'S THE WAY IT IS (1970)

M.G.M.
Documentary
Producer *Dale Hutchinson*
Director *Denis Sanders*

Songs

In rehearsal: Words; The Next Step Is Love; Polk Salad Annie; Cryin' Time; That's Alright; Little Sister; What'd I Say; Stranger In The Crowd; How The Web Was Woven; Just Can't Help Believin'; You Don't Have To Say You Love Me; Bridge Over Troubled Water; Loving Feeling; Mary In The Morning
On stage: Mystery Train/Tiger Man; That's Alright; I've Lost You; Patch It Up; Love Me Tender; Loving Feeling; Sweet Caroline; Just Can't Help Believin'; Bridge Over Troubled Water; One Night; Heartbreak Hotel; Blue Suede Shoes; All Shook Up; Suspicious Minds; Can't Help Fallin'

Musicians

James Burton, John Wilkinson, Charlie Hodge — guitars; Jerry Scheff — bass; Glen Hardin — piano; Ronnie Tutt — drums; Millie Kirkham — vocals; Imperial Quartet, Sweet Inspirations

Synopsis

This is a documentary record of Elvis's triumphant return to live performing. The cameras follow him from rehearsal at an M.G.M. sound stage through two concerts in Las Vegas (August) and Phoenix (September) in 1970. In addition, it shows something of the Elvis phenomenon by covering the 1970 Fan Convention in Luxembourg and interviewing loyal devotees. He is seen relaxed and fooling as he practices, tensing as the build-up for the first night increases and regally superb as his electrifying stage act is captured for posterity on celluloid.

Reviews

This was probably the most enthusiastically received Presley movie of them all. Critics who had deplored his acting, now drooled over his performing; reviewers who dismissed him in a dozen stereotyped roles now went into raptures over the one part he had always played best — Elvis, The King. "Triumphant" was the aptest adjective of all. But to some who had waited nearly 20 years for just such a portrait the movie, almost inevitably, held its disappointments. One of the fans' own correspondents noted: "It should have been ten times better . . . This is not a candid documentary of the personal or working Elvis, but a glossy, cheaply-made, commercially successful 108 minutes with some truthful moments and plenty of songs to cheer the demanding follower."

ELVIS ON TOUR *(1972)*

M.G.M.
Documentary
Producer | *Pierre Adidge*
Director | *Robert Abel*

Songs — Johnny B Goode; See See Rider; Polk Salad Annie; Proud Mary; Never Bin To Spain; Burning Love; Don't Be Cruel; Ready Teddy; Love Me Tender; Bridge Over Troubled Water; Funny How Time Slips Away; An American Trilogy; I Got A Woman; Big Hunk Of Love; You Gave Me A Mountain; Lawdy Miss Clawdy; Can't Help Falling In Love; Separate Ways; For The Good Times; Lead Me Guide Me; Bosom Of Abraham; I John; That's All Right Mama; Mystery Train; Suspicious Minds; Memories. Sweet Sweet Spirit and The Lighthouse sung by Stamps

Musicians — *James Burton — lead guitar; Charlie Hodge — guitar and vocals; Ronnie Tutt — drums; Glen Hardin — piano; Jerry Scheff — bass; John Wilkinson — rhythm guitar; orchestra*

conducted by Joe Guercio
The Sweet Inspirations; J D Sumner & The Stamps; Kathy Westmoreland

Vocalists

Synopsis — This is the documentary record of four dates played on a tour of fifteen concerts in April 1972. It takes *That's The Way It Is* one step further and shows Elvis move his show from the rarified atmosphere of Vegas and similar venues and out to the people. It gives a glimpse of the private man and shows the power of performance and depth of talent that have made him, deservedly, a legend.

Reviews — *That's The Way It Is* showed plainly which Elvis the critics like best and it was undoubtedly as a result of the critical and commercial success of that movie that this one was released. Perhaps the impact of this and the previous documentary were best summed up by one commentator who wrote: "Here is the proof, if any were needed, that while Presley may have failed to gain the throne of Hollywood, he is still King in his own country."

DISC BY DISC

US SINGLES   *All released on RCA unless otherwise indicated.*

1954
That's All Right (Mama)/Blue Moon Of Kentucky *(Sun)*
Good Rockin' Tonight/I Don't Care If The Sun Don't Shine *(Sun)*

1955
Milkcow Blues Boogie/You're A Heartbreaker *(Sun)*
I'm Left, You're Right, She's Gone/Baby, Let's Play House *(Sun)*
Mystery Train/I Forgot To Remember To Forget *(Sun)*
Mystery Train/I Forgot To Remember To Forget
That's All Right (Mama)/Blue Moon Of Kentucky
Good Rockin' Tonight/I Don't Care If The Sun Don't Shine
Milkcow Blues Boogie/You're A Heartbreaker
I'm Left, You're Right, She's Gone/Baby, Let's Play House

1956
Heartbreak Hotel/I Was The One
I Want You, I Need You, I Love You/My Baby Left Me
Hound Dog/Don't Be Cruel
Blue Suede Shoes/Tutti Frutti
I'm Counting On You/I Got A Woman
I'll Never Let You Go/I'm Gonna Sit Right Down And Cry Over You
Tryin' To Get To You/I Love You Because
Blue Moon/Just Because
Money Honey/One-Sided Love Affair
Shake, Rattle And Roll/Lawdy, Miss Clawdy
Love Me Tender/Any Way You Want Me

1957
Too Much/Playing For Keeps
All Shook Up/That's When Your Heartaches Begin
Teddy Bear/Loving You
Jailhouse Rock/Treat Me Nice
Don't/I Beg Of You

1958
Wear My Ring Around Your Neck/Doncha' Think It's Time
Hard Headed Woman/Don't Ask Me Why
I Got Stung/One Night

1959
A Fool Such As I/I Need Your Love Tonight
A Big Hunk O' Love/My Wish Came True

1960
Stuck On You/Fame And Fortune
It's Now Or Never/A Mess Of Blues
Are You Lonesome Tonight/I Gotta Know

1961
Surrender/Lonely Man
I Feel So Bad/Wild In The Country
Little Sister/His Latest Flame
Can't Help Falling In Love/Rock-A-Hula Baby

1962
Good Luck Charm/Anything That's Part Of You
She's Not You/Just Tell Her Jim Said Hello
Return To Sender/Where Do You Come From

1963
One Broken Heart For Sale/They Remind Me Too Much Of You
(You're The) Devil In Disguise/Please Don't Drag That String Around
Bossa Nova Baby/Witchcraft
Kissin' Cousins/It Hurts Me

1964
Kiss Me Quick/Suspicion
Viva Las Vegas/What'd I Say
Such A Night/Never Ending
Ain't That Loving You, Baby/Ask Me
Blue Christmas/Wooden Heart

1965
Do The Clam/You'll Be Gone
Crying In The Chapel/I Believe In The Man In The Sky
(Such An) Easy Question/It Feels So Right

I'm Yours/(It's A) Lonely Highway
Puppet On A String/Wooden Heart
Blue Christmas/Santa Claus Is Back In Town

1966
Tell Me Why/Blue River
Joshua Fit The Battle/Known Only To Him
Milky White Way/Swing Down Sweet Chariot
Frankie And Johnny/Please Don't Stop Loving Me
Love Letters/Come What May
Spinout/All That I Am
If Every Day Was Like Christmas/How Would You Like To Be

1967
Indescribably Blue/Fools Fall In Love
Long Legged Girl (With The Short Dress On)/That's Someone You Never Forget
There's Always Me/Judy
Big Boss Man/You Don't Know Me

1968
Guitar Man/High Heel Sneakers
US Male/Stay Away, Joe
You'll Never Walk Alone/We Call On Him
Let Yourself Go/Your Time Hasn't Come Yet, Baby
A Little Less Conversation/Almost In Love
If I Can Dream/Edge Of Reality

1969
Memories/Charro
How Great Thou Art/His Hand In Mine
In The Ghetto/Any Day Now

Clean Up Your Own Back Yard/The Fair Is
Moving On
Suspicious Minds/You'll Think Of Me
Don't Cry, Daddy/Rubberneckin'
1970 Kentucky Rain/My Little Friend
Mama Liked The Roses/The Wonder Of You
I've Lost You/The Next Step Is Love
You Don't Have To Say You Love Me/Patch It
Up
Rags To Riches/Where Did They Go Lord
1971 Life/Only Believe
I'm Leavin'/Heart Of Rome
It's Only Love/The Sound Of Your Cry
Merry Christmas Baby/O Come All Ye Faithful
1972 Until It's Time For You To Go/We Can Make The
Morning
He Touched Me/Bosom Of Abraham
An American Trilogy/The First Time I Ever Saw
Your Face
Burning Love/It's A Matter Of Time
Separate Ways/Always On My Mind
1973 Fool/Steamroller Blues
Raised On Rock/For Ol' Times Sake
1974 Take Good Care Of Her/I've Got A Thing About
You Baby
Help Me/If You Talk In Your Sleep
It's Midnight/Promised
1975 My Boy/Thinking About You
T-R-O-U-B-L-E/Mr. Songman
Bringing It Back/Pieces Of My Life

UK SINGLES *All released on RCA unless otherwise indicated.*

1956 Heartbreak Hotel/I Was The One *(HMV)*
Blue Suede Shoes/Tutti Frutti *(HMV)*
I Want You, I Need You, I Love You/My Baby
Left Me *(HMV)*
Hound Dog/Don't Be Cruel *(HMV)*
Blue Moon/I Don't Care If The Sun Don't Shine
(HMV)
Love Me Tender/Anyway You Want Me *(HMV)*
1957 Love Me/Mystery Train *(HMV)*
Mystery Train/I Forgot To Remember To Forget
(HMV)
Baby Let's Play House/Rip It Up *(HMV)*
Playin' For Keeps/Too Much *(HMV)*
All Shook Up/That's When Your Heartaches
Begin *(HMV)*
Paralysed/When My Blue Moon Turns To Gold
(HMV)
Lawdy, Miss Clawdy/Tryin' To Get To You
(HMV)
Loving You/Teddy Bear
Gotta Lotta Livin' To Do/Party
Santa Bring My Baby Back/Santa Claus Is Back
In Town
1958 I'm Left, You're Right, She's Gone/How Do You
Think I Feel *(HMV)*
Jailhouse Rock/Treat Me Nice *(HMV)*
I Beg Of You/Don't *(HMV)*
Wear My Ring Around Your Neck/Dontcha
Think It's Time *(HMV)*
Hard Headed Woman/Don't Ask Me Why *(HMV)*
King Creole/Dixieland Rock *(HMV)*
All Shook Up/Heartbreak Hotel *(HMV)*
Hound Dog/Blue Suede Shoes *(HMV)*
1959 One Night/I Got Stung
A Fool Such As I/I Need Your Love Tonight
A Big Hunk Of Love/My Wish Came True
1960 Stuck On You/Fame And Fortune
A Mess Of Blues/The Girl Of My Best Friend
It's Now Or Never/Make Me Know It
1961 I Gotta Know/Are You Lonesome Tonight
Wooden Heart/Tonight Is So Right For Love
Surrender/Lonely Man

Wild In The Country/I Feel So Bad
His Latest Flame/Little Sister
1962 Rock-A-Hula Baby/I Can't Help Falling In Love
Good Luck Charm/Anything That' Part Of You
She's Not You/Just Tell Her Jim Said Hello
Return To Sender/Where Do You Come From
1963 One Broken Heart For Sale/They Remind Me
Too Much Of You
Devil In Disguise/Please Don't Drag That String
Around
Bossa Nova Baby/Witchcraft
Kiss Me Quick/Something Blue
1964 Viva Las Vegas/What'd I Say
Kissin' Cousins/It Hurts Me
Such A Night/Never Ending
Ain't That Loving You Baby/Ask Me
Blue Christmas/White Christmas
1965 Do The Clam/You'll Be Gone
Crying In The Chapel/I Believe In The Man In
The Sky
Tell Me Why/Puppet On A String
Blue River/Do Not Disturb
1966 Please Don't Stop Loving Me/Frankie And
Johnny
Love Letters/Come What May
All That I Am/Spin Out
If Every Day Was Like Xmas/How Would You
Like To Be
1967 Indescribably Blue/Fools Fall In Love
The Love Machine/You Gotta Stop
Long Legged Girl (With The Short Dress
On)/That's Someone You'll Never Forget
There's Always Me/Judy
Big Boss Man/You Don't Know Me
1968 Guitar Man/High Heel Sneakers
US Male/Stay Away
You'll Never Walk Alone/We Call On Him
A Little Less Conversation/Almost In Love
1969 If I Can Dream/Memories
In The Ghetto/Any Day Now
Clean Up Your Own Backyard/The Fair's
Moving On
Suspicious Minds/You'll Think Of Me
Don't Cry Daddy/Rubberneckin'
1970 Kentucky Rain/My Little Friend
The Wonder Of You/Mama Liked The Roses
I've Lost You/The Next Step Is Love
1971 You Don't Have To Say/Patch It Up
There Goes My Everything/I Really Don't Want
To Know
Rags To Riches/Where Did They Go Lord
Heartbreak Hotel/Hound Dog/Don't Be Cruel
(maxi)
I'm Leaving/Heart Of Rome
Jailhouse Rock/Are You Lonesome
Tonight/Teddy Bear/Steadfast, Loyal, True
(maxi)
I Just Can't Help Believing/How The Web Was
Woven
1972 Until It's Time For You To Go/We Can Make The
Morning
American Trilogy/The First Time Ever I Saw
Your Face
Burning Love/It's A Matter Of Time
Separate Ways/Always On My Mind
1973 Polk Salad Annie/See See Rider
Fool/Steamroller Blues
Raised On Rock/For Ol' Times Sake
1974 My Boy/Loving Arms
1975 Promised Land/It's Midnight
Green Green Grass Of Home/Thinking About
You
T-r-o-u-b-l-e/Mr. Songman
Blue Moon/You're A Heartbreaker/I'm Left,
You're Right, She's Gone (maxi)

US ALBUMS *All released on RCA unless otherwise indicated*

1956	Elvis Presley
	Elvis
1957	Loving You
	Elvis' Christmas Album
1958	Elvis' Gold Records
	King Creole
1959	For LP Fans Only
	A Date With Elvis
	Elvis' Gold Records Vol. 2
1960	Elvis Is Back
	GI Blues
	His Hand In Mine
1961	Something For Everybody
	Blue Hawaii
1962	Pot Luck
	Girls! Girls! Girls!
1963	It Happened At The World's Fair
	Elvis' Golden Records, Vol 3
	Fun In Acapulco
1964	Kissin' Cousins
	Roustabout
1965	Girl Happy
	Elvis For Everyone
	Harum Scarum
1966	Frankie And Johnny
	Paradise, Hawaiian Style
	Spinout
1967	How Great Thou Art
	Double Trouble
	Clambake
1968	Elvis' Gold Records, Vol. 4
	Speedway
	Elvis Singing Flaming Star And Others
	Elvis
1969	Elvis Sings Flaming Star *(Camden)*
	From Elvis In Memphis
	From Memphis To Vegas/From Vegas To Memphis (2 record set)
1970	On Stage: February 1970
	In Person At The International Hotel
	Let's Be Friends *(Camden)*
	Worldwide 50 Gold Award Hits, Vol 1
	Elvis' Christmas Album *(Camden)*
	Almost In Love *(Camden)*
	Back In Memphis
	Elvis: That's The Way It Is
1971	Elvis Country
	You'll Never Walk Alone *(Camden)*
	Love Letters From Elvis
	C'Mon Everybody *(Camden)*
	Elvis: The Other Sides — Worldwide Gold Award Hits, Vol 2
	I Got Lucky *(Camden)*
	The Wonderful World Of Christmas
1972	Elvis—Now
	Elvis Sings Hits From His Movies, Vol 1
	He Touched Me *(Camden)*
	"Burning Love" And Hits From His Movies, Vol. 2 *(Camden)*
	Elvis As Recorded Live At Madison Square Garden (June 10, 1972)
	Separate Ways *(Camden)*
1973	Aloha From Hawaii Via Satellite (January 14, 1973)
	ELVIS
	Raised On Rock/For Ol' Times Sake
1974	ELVIS: A Legendary Performer, Vol. 1
	Good Times
	Elvis As Recorded Live On Stage In Memphis
	Having Fun With Elvis On Stage
1975	Promised Land
	Elvis: Pure Gold *(Camden)*
	Today

UK ALBUMS *All released on RCA unless otherwise indicated.*

1956 Rock 'N' Roll No. 1 *(HMV)*
1957 Rock 'N' Roll No. 2 *(HMV)*
      The Best Of Elvis *(HMV)*
      Loving You
      Elvis's Christmas Album
1958 King Creole
      Elvis Golden Records
1959 Elvis
      A Date With Elvis
1960 Elvis Gold Records (Vol. 2)
      Elvis Is Back
      GI Blues
      His Hand In Mine
1961 Something For Everybody
      Blue Hawaii
1962 Pot Luck With Elvis
1963 Rock 'N' Roll No. 2
      Girls! Girls! Girls!
      It Happened At The World's Fair
      Fun In Acapulco
1964 Elvis's Golden Records (Vol. 3)
      Kissin' Cousins
      Roustabout
1965 Girl Happy
      Flaming Star And Summer Kisses
      Elvis For Everyone
1966 Harem Holiday
      Frankie And Johnny
      Paradise, Hawaiian Style
      California Holiday
      How Great Thou Art
1967 Double Trouble
1968 Clambake
      Elvis Gold Records (Vol. 4)
      Speedway
1969 Elvis Sings Flaming Star
      Elvis
      From Elvis In Memphis
1970 Let's Be Friends
      From Memphis To Vegas/From Vegas To
      Memphis
      On Stage
      Elvis Christmas Album
      Worldwide 50 Gold Award Hits (Vol. 1)
      Almost In Love
1971 That's The Way It Is
      You'll Never Walk Alone
      Elvis Country (I'm 10,000 Years Old)
      C'Mon Everybody
      Love Letters
      The Other Sides — Worldwide Gold
      Award Hits (Vol. 2)
      Wonderful World Of Xmas
      I Got Lucky
1972 ''Elvis — Now!''
      He Touched Me
      Live At Madison Square Garden
      Elvis Sings Hits From His Movies (Vol. 1)
      Burning Love And Hits From His Movies
      (Vol. 2)
1973 Aloha From Hawaii Via Satellite
      Separate Ways
      Elvis
1974 Having Fun On Stage With Elvis
      Hits Of The 70's
      Live On Stage In Memphis
      A Legendary Performer
      Promised Land
      Elvis' 40 Greatest *(Arcade)*
1975 Elvis Today
      Easy Come, Easy Go
      Elvis — US Male
      The Sun Collection